by William Inge

FOUR PLAYS
Come Back, Little Sheba
Picnic
Bus Stop
The Dark at the Top of the Stairs

A LOSS OF ROSES

SUMMER BRAVE AND ELEVEN SHORT PLAYS

SUMMER BRAVE

and Eleven Short Plays

*SUMMER BRAVE

BRAVE

and Eleven Short Plays

WILLIAM INGE

Random House   *New York*

The Mall was first published in Esquire, issue of January 1959.

Library of Congress Catalog Card Number: 62-12730

Design by Ruth Smerechniak

Manufactured in the United States of America

For Helene

Preface

It wouldn't be fair to say that *Summer Brave* is the original version of *Picnic*. I have written before that I never completely fulfilled my original intentions in writing *Picnic* before we went into production with the play back in 1953, and that I wrote what some considered a fortuitous ending in order to have a finished play to go into rehearsal. A couple of years after *Picnic* had closed on Broadway, after the film version had made its success, I got the early version out of my files and began to rework it, just for my own satisfaction. *Summer Brave* is the result. The title is from a poem of Shakespeare's, "Age like winter weather; Youth like summer brave." I admit that I prefer it to the version of the play that was produced, but I don't necessarily expect others to agree. *Summer Brave* might not have enjoyed any success on Broadway whatever, nor won any of the prizes that were bestowed upon *Picnic.* But I feel that it is more humorously true than *Picnic,* and it does fulfill my original intentions.

Of the one-act plays in this volume, *To Bobolink, for Her Spirit* is the earliest, having been written in 1949. The others all were written in the early 1950's. *People in the Wind* may be recognized as the embryo of *Bus Stop.*

Bus Riley's Back in Town is a play I happen to be working on now in expanded form. *The Boy in the Basement,* which may seem very sketchy in its present form, is a play I hope to do more with in the future. *The Strains of Triumph, The Tiny Closet,* and *The Mall* seem to me complete in their present form and will doubtless remain just as they are. The other pieces are fragments or sketches that I have written in exploration of characters in larger works that I may or may not develop in the future.

WILLIAM INGE

Contents

SUMMER
BRAVE

*The rewritten and final version
of the romantic comedy PICNIC*

Youth like summer morn, age like winter weather;

Youth like summer brave, age like winter bare.

"The Passionate Pilgrim"

SHAKESPEARE

Act One

The action of the play takes place on the front porch and lawn of a small frame house in a small Kansas town. The house itself is a humble dwelling built with no other pretension than to provide shelter for its occupants, but its occupants are women who have worked hard to keep up an appearance; so the house, although it may need a coat of paint, is kept tidy, and there are colorful slip covers on the porch furniture and lush flower beds at the edge of the porch. Surrounding the house are clusters of heavy foliage from the trees and a stretch of green lawn that levels back, fading into the horizon. It is a homey scene marred only by a sign, hand-painted, tacked to one of the thin little columns on the porch: ROOMERS.

In the background can be seen the back entrance to the house of a neighbor, MRS. POTTS, who inhabits a cozy cottage. Beyond that is the panorama of a typical, small Midwestern town, with a church steeple, a grain elevator, a great silo in the center of a cattle ranch, and a few municipal buildings rising out of the sloping terrain.

When the curtain goes up it is early morning and the stage is empty. It is late summer, Labor Day, and autumn has just begun to edge the green landscape with a rim of brown. The scene has the color of luscious fruit just beginning to ripen. Dew is still on the countryside, and mist rises from the earth in the distance. Far off, the

*whistle of a train coming to town is heard. It is a happy,
promising sound. Then* MILLIE OWENS *comes bursting
out of the door of the front house, wiping her breakfast
off her mouth. She is a girl of sixteen, full of the electric
vitality of adolescence. She is not pretty because obviously she does not think of herself as pretty, although her
features and coloring are good. She would seem to prefer
to flaunt her independence of prettiness, and to be quer-
ulous and scrappy. She wears boys' dungarees, sneakers
and a denim shirt. It is her secret habit to come to the
porch in the morning to smoke her after-breakfast cigarette. She is just lighting up when the* NEWSBOY *comes
by and slings a paper at the house. He is a well fed, Midwestern youth, just verging on maturity. He seems to
have a desire to tease* MILLIE. *She assails him.*

MILLIE   Hey, crazy! wanta knock the house down?

NEWSBOY   I don't hear you.

MILLIE   If you ever break a window you'll hear me.

NEWSBOY   Go back to bed!

MILLIE   Go blow your nose!

NEWSBOY   Go back to bed and tell your pretty sister to
come out. 'Sno fun lookin' at *you.*
(MILLIE *glares at him resentfully as he saunters off,
whistling and folding his papers. She sits on the doorstep, unfolds the paper and looks at the headlines.
Then* BOMBER *and* BEANO *seem to spring onto the
stage,* BEANO *running first to the porch to deliver two
quarts of milk, then joining* BOMBER *in an exhibitionistic display of gymnastics. They turn somersaults and
walk on their hands with almost professional grace*)

MILLIE   What do you crazy guys think you're doin'?

BOMBER   Havin' fun. What's it t'you?

MILLIE   You can go have your fun somewhere else.

BOMBER   Kill-joy!

BEANO   Goonface!

MILLIE   (*Doubling her fists and going after them*)   You take that back. No one calls me that and gets away with it. You ornery bastards, I'll kill you.

BOMBER   (*Holding* MILLIE'S *fists with easy assertion of masculine superiority*)   Cut it out, Madam Tar-zan.

BEANO   (*To* BOMBER)   She cusses just like a man.

BOMBER   Where's your good-lookin' sister?

BEANO   Yah, where is she? Lyin' around in her bood-war?

MILLIE   Madge wouldn't spit on a couple of jerks like you.

BOMBER   Oh! She wouldn't?

BEANO   Just 'cause she's pretty, I guess she spits per-fume.

MILLIE   You're just supposed to deliver the milk and save your wise remarks.

BEANO   *I* seen her ridin' around in Seymour's big Cadil-lac, makin' out like she's a movie star.

BOMBER   You can tell your good-lookin' sister, Bomber Gutzell don't need no Cadillac to show a girl a good time.

BEANO   (*Picking it up in his more or less goofy way*)   Come on, Madge! I wanta show you a good time, baby! What d'ya say, Madge? Wanta have a good time? (*To their surprise,* MADGE *appears in the doorway. The boys gulp,* MADGE *is beautiful and they cannot continue their crude joking in her presence, for they stand in awe of her beauty*)

MADGE   Who's making so much noise?

MILLIE   These juvenile delinquents!

BOMBER   Gee, Madge, I hope we didn't wake you.

BEANO   Hi, Madge!

MADGE   (*Sullen*)   What do you want?

BOMBER   (*Serious now*)   Hey, Madge, a bunch of us guys are chippin' in on a hot rod, radio and everything. I get it every Friday night. How 'bout it, Madge?

BEANO   I get it every Tuesday, Madge.

MADGE   I'm not one of those girls that jumps in a hot rod every time you boys turn a corner and *honk*. If a boy wants a date with *me,* he can come to a door like a gentleman, and ring the bell, and ask if I'm *in.*

BEANO   (*To* BOMBER)   Who does she think she is?

MILLIE   (*Casually superior*)   Madge goes steady with Alan Seymour. He sends her flowers every time they go out.

BOMBER   I can't send you any flowers, baby, but I can *send* you.

MILLIE   Listen to him braggin'.

BEANO   Let me pick you up some night after Seymour brings you home, Madge. He'll never know the difference.

MADGE   (*Quite aloof*)   I don't go out with other boys. Everyone in town knows that.

BOMBER   Yah, you like ridin' around in Seymour's big Cadillac, feelin' like Mrs. Richbitch.

MADGE   I'm sure I never heard of the lady so I couldn't possibly know who you are referring to.
(*The sound of* ALAN SEYMOUR'S *car is heard*)

BEANO   (*Grabbing* BOMBER *by the arm*)   Hey, here comes Seymour!

BOMBER   I can handle Seymour. Come on, Madge!

BEANO   Come on, Bomber. She's too stuck on herself to give a guy a break.

MADGE   (*Angrily stomping a foot*)   That's not so.

BOMBER   It ain't fair, a gal as good-lookin' as you, not givin' a guy a break. It ain't fair.
(BEANO *pulls* BOMBER *off*)

MILLIE   (*Getting the last word*)   Go back to your milk route.

MADGE   I'm *not* stuck on myself. Those boys make me mad.

MILLIE   (*Calling*)   Hi, Alan!

ALAN   (*Coming on. He is a pleasant-looking young man, just out of college. Cautiously dressed, well bred*)   Hi, Millie!

MADGE   (*Kidding him*)   Did you come by to take me to work?

ALAN   No.

MADGE   I bet you forgot it's a holiday. I bet anything you forgot.

ALAN   I never forget.
(*He hands her a bouquet of flowers*)

MADGE   (*Taking the flowers*)   Oh, aren't they pretty!

ALAN   I thought you might like to wear them to the picnic tonight.

MADGE   Millie, take them out to the refrigerator for me.

MILLIE   Who was your servant this time last year?

MADGE   (*A quick comeback*)   I made your bed this morning.

MILLIE   Oh, be quiet!

MADGE   I have to make it every morning if I want the room to look decent.

MILLIE   Save your breath. (*Takes the flowers*) We goin' swimmin' this afternoon, Alan?

ALAN   Sure.

MILLIE   (*Going inside*)   Oh boy!

MADGE   (*Yawns and stretches*)   Gee, it's good to sleep late on Monday morning.

ALAN   I've done a day's work already.

MADGE   But this is a holiday.

ALAN   Dad wanted me to drive out to his farms and collect the rents. I don't mind. I like to work.

MADGE   You're pretty unusual.

ALAN   But I do. Every morning at college, I was up at six-thirty to do my studying. You can lose yourself in work just as well as you can having fun.

MADGE   Lose yourself?

ALAN   Sure . . . when other things go wrong.

MADGE   What other things?

ALAN   Oh . . . I don't know.

MADGE   What?

ALAN   Well . . . I never had much fun in college like the other fellows did.

MADGE   Why not?

ALAN   I don't know.

MADGE   With all those beautiful college girls?

ALAN   (*Very tenderly now*)   Madge, I never even hoped to find a girl as lovely as you.

MADGE   (*Touched*)   Honest?

ALAN   At school, I didn't even *think* of the pretty girls. They were always so popular and there were always so many other fellows trying to get dates. I just kept my mind on my studies.

MADGE   (*Tenderly*)   You're the nicest boy I know.

ALAN   Madge, you're so beautiful, I can't believe you're mine. Every morning, I wake up and pinch myself to see if I'm dreaming.

MADGE   You're joking.

ALAN   I'm not. Even when I pinch myself, I can't be-lieve it. Something'll happen, I say. She'll disappear. She isn't real.

MADGE   (*A little fearful*)   Alan, don't say that.

ALAN   I was joking.

MADGE   It bothers me.

ALAN   Why?

MADGE   Because . . .

ALAN   I don't care if you're real or not. I love you.

MADGE   Just the same . . . I'm real.

(FLO *comes out on the porch. She is a wiry little woman in her mid-forties who has had to function for the last ten years both as mother and father to the girls, so she has a spirited independence. She carries a dress over one arm and a sewing basket*)

FLO (*She always gives* ALAN *her cheeriest greeting*) Well, good morning, Alan! I didn't expect to find you here so early. Have you had your breakfast?

ALAN Yes, thank you.

FLO There'll be a big crowd at the park tonight. Maybe you'd better reserve a table for us. Get one by the river, if you can, close to a Dutch oven.

ALAN All right.

FLO Have you found a date for Millie?

MADGE Mom, Millie doesn't like boys.

FLO She'll find a boy she likes one of these days. There'll be dancing at the park tonight. It's a shame Millie doesn't have a young man to take her. Isn't there *anyone* you can find?

ALAN Well, I . . .

MADGE Alan went to college, Mom. He doesn't know any of the boys in town.

FLO Boys in town are a worthless lot. Maybe Millie's better off without a date.

ALAN Want to come with me, Madge?

FLO Madge, you'll have to try on your dress if I'm ever going to finish it.

MADGE Can't I try it on this afternoon?

FLO This afternoon I have to fry the chickens. Oh, Alan, would you go to the poultry house for me? (*She digs in her pocket for money*)

ALAN   Let *me* buy them, Mrs. Owens.

FLO   No, this party is on Helen Potts and me. (*Gives him the money*) They said the chickens'd be ready.

ALAN   See you all later.
(*He goes off*)

MADGE   'Bye, Alan!

FLO   (*Watching him depart*)   My! I wish I'd known a boy like him when I was a girl.

MADGE   I think Alan has an inferiority complex.

FLO   When his father's a banker?

MADGE   *Any*one can have an inferiority complex, didn't you know that?

FLO   No!

MADGE   They say even Elizabeth Taylor has one.

FLO   He's a fine young man, and he's head over heels in love with you.

MADGE   Mom, when we go to a movie, he just sits there holding my hand. He doesn't even watch the picture. I get kinda embarrassed.

FLO   You're pretty. Of course he wants to look at you. Come try on your dress.

MADGE   I just washed my hair.

FLO   Then hold it in front of you so I can check the hem. (MADGE *obeys*) Young men like Alan don't grow on trees. You better get busy.

MADGE   Mom, sometimes I think I'd like a career.

FLO   What kind of a career?

MADGE   Alan says if I'd gone away to college and joined a big sorority, I'd have won the beauty contest.

FLO   I can't send you to college.

MADGE   Millie's going.

FLO   Millie won herself a scholarship.

MADGE   And I was too dumb.

FLO   Now, Madge . . . You don't need college the way Millie does.

MADGE   I bet if I went to New York or Chicago, I could get a job as a model and those jobs pay lots of money.

FLO   Nonsense!

MADGE   Or I could even go on the stage.

FLO   What would you do on the stage?

MADGE   (*Giving her version of a parading showgirl*) Walk back and forth, wearing jewels and furs, smiling at people.

FLO   Come back here and quit posing.

MADGE   (*Angry*)   I'm not posing.

FLO   You pose like a duchess all day long. Your father spoiled you, carrying you on his shoulder, all over the neighborhood, for people to brag about.

MADGE   You blame everything on Dad.

FLO   Now I make you one pretty dress after another, then you pose some more. Get busy, girl. Think of the future. The future's not going to think of *you*.

MADGE   I'm only eighteen.

FLO   And next summer you'll be nineteen, then twenty, then twenty-one. And then the years'll start going so fast you'll lose count of 'em. First thing you know, you'll be forty, still selling candy at the dime store.

MADGE   You don't have to get morbid.

(*Suddenly* HAL CARTER *appears at the edge of the porch. He is an exceedingly handsome and virile youth in his early twenties, dressed only in dungarees and cowboy boots, having stripped off his shirt to work in the sun. His torso is muscular and shapely. But he is a youth who takes his body for granted so there is nothing exhibitionistic in his unconscious physical display*)

HAL   Pardon me, ma'm, but was that Al Seymour just drove off in the Ford?

FLO   (*Surprised*)   Why . . . yes.

HAL   I thought that was Al. I wasn't sure.

FLO   (*A little dubious*)   Do you know Alan?

HAL   Al, he's about the best friend I ever had.
(MADGE, *seated on the doorstep, is not directly in* HAL'S *view, but she is managing to get a few looks at him*)

FLO   Is that so?

HAL   Yah! We went to school together. Well, I'm afraid I didn't go to school *much,* but Al did. Al, he helped me with my studies, but it didn't do much good. I left after the football season ended.

FLO   He'll be back later.

HAL   Will his face fall when he sees *me!* Gee, I wanta see Al.
(*He wanders back to his work.* FLO *stands and goes to the edge of the porch watching him*)

FLO   Now who is that?

MADGE   He musta been at Mrs. Potts' for breakfast.

FLO   A tramp?

MADGE   Can't he eat his breakfast at Mrs. Potts' without being a tramp?

FLO   I don't believe he was a friend of Alan's.

MADGE   I don't see why not.

FLO   He isn't a young man of Alan's caliber.

MADGE   You just don't like him.

FLO   It disturbs a woman . . . to have a man suddenly appear like that . . . out of the blue.

MADGE   I know why you didn't like him. I bet anything I know.

FLO   Why?

MADGE   *You* know why!

FLO   (*Embarrassed*)   Well . . .

MADGE   Confess!

FLO   Well, it seems to me he could have put on a shirt before addressing two strange women.

MADGE   (*Smirking a little*)   I thought that was the reason.
(MADGE *considers this very funny and giggles.* FLO *is confused*)

FLO   Hold the dress up again.
(MADGE *does so.* MILLIE *kicks open the screen door and comes out gnawing an apple, looking truculent*)

MILLIE   Everyone around here gets to dress up and goes places 'ceptin' me.

FLO   Alan's trying to find you a date to the dance tonight.

MILLIE   I don't want Alan asking any of these crazy boys in town to take me any place.

MADGE   Beggars can't be choosers.

MILLIE   (*Angry*)   You shut up.

FLO   Madge, that was mean.

MADGE   I don't care. If she wants a date, why doesn't she dress up and act decent.

MILLIE   Because I'm gonna dress and act the way I want to. That's why. And if you don't like it, you know what you can do.

MADGE   (*Almost under her breath*)   . . . always complaining because she doesn't have any friends . . . and she smells so bad people don't wanta be near her.

MILLIE   I hate you.

FLO   Girls!

MILLIE   (*Mockingly*)   La-de-da! Madge is the *pretty* one. Madge puts on lipstick and looks in the mirror to see how pretty she is . . . but she's so dumb they almost had to burn the school house down to get *her* out of it.

MADGE   (*Hotly*)   That's not so.

MILLIE   Oh, isn't it? You never would have graduated if it hadn't been for Jumpin' Jeeter.

FLO   Who's Jumpin' Jeeter?

MILLIE   Professor Jeeter. Teaches history. Kids call him Jumpin' Jeeter 'cause he's so jumpy with all the pretty girls in his classes. He was *flunking* Madge . . . till she went in to see him after school . . . and she *cried* . . . and said . . . (*Mockingly*) she just didn't know what she'd do if she didn't pass history.

MADGE (*Blushing with embarrassment*) Mom, she's
making that up.

MILLIE   Like fun I am!

MADGE (*Embarrassed now to tears*)   Millie, I *hate* you.

FLO (*Interceding*)   Girls! Girls!

MADGE (*Sobbing*)   Just because I have a little pride and
you go around looking like a scarecrow.

MILLIE   I'd rather improve my brains than my kisser,
moron!

MADGE   Goon!

MILLIE (*Enraged*) Madge, you slut! Take that back
or I'll kill you.
(*She goes after* MADGE *with her fists*)

FLO   Girls! Stop it this instant. What'll the neighbors
say?

MLLIE   No one can call me "goon" and get by with it.

FLO   You called her *worse* names.

MILLIE   It doesn't hurt what names I call *her*. She's
pretty, so names don't hurt her at all. She's pretty, so
nothing else matters.
(*She goes inside crying, letting the door slam behind
her*)

FLO (*Personally to Madge*)   Be careful how you talk
to the child.

MADGE   You always take her side.

FLO   I feel sorry for Millie.

MADGE   You never feel sorry for *me*.

FLO   I would if there was any reason.

MADGE (*With an edge of self-pity*)   You think more of
  her than you do of me.

FLO (*Decisive*)   Madge, that's not so!

MADGE   You talk like it at times.

FLO   You were the first born and your father thought
  the sun rose and set in *you*. Things were changed by
  the time Millie was born.

MADGE (*Cautiously*)   Mom, did you love Dad?

FLO   What a question!

MADGE   I'm serious.

FLO   Well . . .

MADGE   Did you?

FLO   Well, of course I did!

MADGE   I don't see why it's so hard to admit it.

FLO   It can be embarrassing to love a man.

MADGE   I don't see why.

FLO   'Cause a man is stronger . . . in most ways . . .
  and the woman is weak to begin with . . . and if she's
  in love with him, she's all the weaker. You have to
  fight for things in this life and . . . sometimes it's a
  disadvantage to be in love.
  (ROSEMARY SYDNEY, *letting the screen door slam be-*
  hind her, makes a sort of cavalier entrance, wearing a
  flowered kimono over her suit skirt and brassière. She
  carries a hand mirror and make-up kit, prepared to
  spend the morning working on her face, massaging it,
  taking care of the blackheads. Her hair now is plas-
  tered to her head in a tight finger wave and her face
  is covered with cold cream. She probably is as old as
  FLO *but would not have anyone know it*)

ROSEMARY   Anyone mind if an old-maid school teacher joins their company?

FLO   Sit down, Rosemary.

ROSEMARY   Shoot! I like a little town like this where you can go around as you please on a day off and nobody gives a darn. (*Sniffs the atmosphere*) I smell smoke.

FLO   A young man over at Helen Potts', burning the trash.

ROSEMARY   Oh!

FLO   If I was Helen Potts, I'd make him put a shirt on.

ROSEMARY   (*Studying Hal*)   I agree.
(*Joining* FLO *at the porch*) The mail come yet?

FLO   No mail today, Rosemary. It's Labor Day.
(MILLIE *wanders out reading a book*)

ROSEMARY   I forgot. I thought I might be gettin' a letter from Eustace. He's the man I met at the high school picnic last year. (*A sudden bawdy laugh, as though it were all terribly funny*) Been wantin' to marry me ever since. A nice fellow and a peck of fun, but I don't have time for any of 'em when they start gettin' serious on me.

FLO   You school teachers are mighty independent.

ROSEMARY   Shoot! I lived this long without a man. I don't see what's to keep me from goin' on without one.

FLO   Be here for lunch today?

ROSEMARY   No. Rowena Bowersock and Mary Lou McCord are having a welcome-home party down at the hotel. Irma Kronkite's comin' by for me, soon as I get my face ready.
(*She is busily massaging her skin*)

FLO   What's that you're rubbin' in?

ROSEMARY   Ponsella Three-way Tissue Cream. It makes a good base for your make-up.

FLO   There was an article in the *Woman's Home Companion* about some girl who got skin poisoning from using all those face creams.

ROSEMARY   Harriet Bristol . . . she's the American History teacher . . . she got ahold of some of that beauty clay last year and it darn near took her skin off. All we girls thought she had leprosy.

MILLIE   (*Out of curiosity, has picked up* MADGE'S *manicure set and begun to experiment*)   Hey! How do you do your right hand?

MADGE   If you were nicer to people, maybe people would do something nice for you sometime.

MILLIE   *I'll* get along.

ROSEMARY   How come, Millie? You got a beau?

MILLIE   (*Emphatically*)   No!

ROSEMARY   You can't kid me. Girls don't bother to paint their fingernails unless they think some boy is gonna take notice.
(*Very indignant,* MILLIE *puts the manicure set aside and resumes her reading*)

MADGE   She likes boys. She just wants to be different.

MILLIE   I wish everyone'd keep their big mouth shut.

FLO   Millie, you should be ashamed to talk that way to Miss Sydney.

ROSEMARY   Shoot! I don't care. Startin' tomorrow, I'll have kids yellin' at me all day. I might as well be gettin' used to it.

MILLIE   I was talkin' to Madge.

FLO   Madge, your hair's dry now. Go inside and try on your dress.

(MADGE *takes the dress and goes inside.* MRS. POTTS *is heard calling from her back porch*)

MRS. POTTS   Flo! Flo!

FLO (*Calling back*)   Come on over, Helen.

MRS. POTTS   Flo, will you be using the clothesline today?

FLO   No! (MRS. POTTS *busies herself in her back yard.* FLO *resumes*) Poor Helen! She has her hands full.

ROSEMARY (*Gossipy*)   Mrs. Owens, why does she call herself *Mrs.* Potts? You said her mother had the marriage annulled.

FLO   She did.

ROSEMARY   How long was she married to the boy?

FLO   A few days.

ROSEMARY   And they never lived together?

FLO   No. Helen's mother kept her locked in a room till the annulment papers came through.

ROSEMARY   I declare!

FLO   That was during the First War. The boy got killed overseas. He left everything he had to Helen. Helen was broken-hearted. She's been using his name ever since. It makes the old lady mad.

ROSEMARY   Mrs. Potts oughta be able to do what she likes. She takes care of the old lady all day long.

FLO   Waits on her hand and foot. She can't leave the house two minutes without the old lady wantin' to know where she is.

ROSEMARY   Shhh! here she comes.

MRS. POTTS   (*Comes hustling on, a dumpy little woman past fifty, given to giggles and gushing enthusiasm. She has retained a baby-doll cuteness and rotundity*) Have you girls seen the handsome young man I've got working for me?

ROSEMARY   I've got better things to do than waste my time lookin' at handsome young men.

FLO   Helen Potts, you're gonna end up dead the way you take in tramps and all sorts of riffraff.

MRS. POTTS   He's *not* a tramp. He's a very nice young man. He went to school with Alan.

FLO   I don't believe that for a second.

MRS. POTTS   That's what he *says*.

MRS. POTTS' MOTHER   (*An aged and cracking voice calls from a distance*)   Helen! Helen!

MRS. POTTS   Oh dear! (*Calls back*) I'm over at Flo's, Mama.

MRS. POTTS' MOTHER   Helen! Helen!

MRS. POTTS   You don't need me, Mama. I'll be back after a while.

FLO   You and your poor old mother there all alone, I think you'd be scared to let strange men in the house.

MRS. POTTS   He stood at the back door smiling. "Please, ma'am, have you got anything good for an empty stomach?" he asks me. Why I wasn't scared at all.

FLO   What'd you feed him?

MRS. POTTS   I fixed some biscuits.

FLO   Helen, you didn't go to all that trouble!

MRS. POTTS   I haven't had occasion to fix biscuits in a long time. A woman should keep in practice. Then I gave him ham and eggs and all the hot coffee he could drink. He saw a piece of cherry pie in the icebox and he wanted that, too. Imagine, cherry pie for breakfast!

ROSEMARY   Young men like him take their sweet things where they find them.

FLO   Seems to me, a young man who amounted to anything would have more pride than to beg his breakfast off a lady.

MRS. POTTS   He's *working* for his breakfast. For months I've wanted the big chiffonier in the front bedroom moved back in Mama's room so I can store sheets in it. I couldn't budge the big, bulky thing. But he's a husky young man. He moved it around like it was made of tissue paper.

FLO   Helen, you let him go upstairs?

MRS. POTTS   Of course!

ROSEMARY   (*Conceiving it all as a bawdy joke*)   Sounds t'me like Mrs. Potts had herself a new boy friend.

MRS. POTTS   (*Injured by the implication*)   I don't think that's very funny.

ROSEMARY   Shoot! Don't pay any attention t'me, Mrs. Potts. I'm just a tease.

FLO   Come on up, Helen.

MRS. POTTS   Well! I s'pose I *could* go back and sit on my own front porch.

FLO   Old widow ladies like us gotta stick together.

MRS. POTTS   But I hate to sit on my own front porch, for neighbors to walk by and see me there all alone. (MADGE *comes out in her new dress, and* MRS. POTTS' *face brightens with admiration*) I like to sit out here where there's young people coming and going.

ROSEMARY (*In a sudden seizure of sincerity*) Mrs. Potts, if I said anything to offend you, I wanta apologize.
(MRS. POTTS *assures her there are no hard feelings*)

FLO (*To* MADGE, *who stands before her now modeling the dress*) How does it feel, Madge?

MADGE (*Tugging at the dress across the hips*) I seem to have grown some since the last dress you made me.

MRS. POTTS Isn't Madge the pretty one! Every time you see her, she's prettier than she was the time before.

FLO (*Beginning to make inspections*) We'll see what we can do.

MRS. POTTS Madge is the pretty one; Millie is the *smart* one. Millie's going to be a great novelist some day. I feel it in my bones. What're you reading, Millie girl?

MILLIE   *The Ballad of the Sad Café.*

ROSEMARY (*Protesting with shock*) Good lord, Mrs. Owens, you let your daughter read filthy books like that?

FLO   Is there anything wrong with the book?

ROSEMARY   Everyone in it is some sort of degenerate.

MILLIE (*Hotly protesting*) That's not so. It's on the reading list of all the colleges.

MRS. POTTS (*Eliminating herself from the argument*) I don't read much.

ROSEMARY   Well, those college professors don't have any morals.

FLO   Millie, give me that book. I'll not have you reading anything immoral.

MILLIE (*Tenaciously*)   No! It's *not* immoral. It's *not!*

FLO   Millie!

MILLIE (*Hugging the book to her bosom*)   You all shut up. This is a wonderful book. You stupid characters don't know what you're talking about.

FLO (*Giving up with Millie*)   Where she comes by her tastes, I don't know.

ROSEMARY   Young people today, they read all sorts of trash.

MADGE   You should see some of the pictures she has in her room.

MILLIE   Those pictures are by Picasso, and he's a great artist.

MADGE (*Derogatorily*)   A picture of a woman with six eyes!

MILLIE   And what have you got on your wall? Pictures of Robert Mitchum and Glenn Ford and Burt Lancaster.

MADGE   They're prettier than Picasso.

ROSEMARY   Lord, that Picasso! Another crazy man! Paints all those wild pictures that don't look like anybody at all.

MRS. POTTS   I saw some of his pictures in *Life* magazine. They weren't very pretty to look at.

MILLIE (*An ultimatum*)   Pictures don't have to be pretty!
(*She goes haughtily inside, letting the door slam. Now there is a sudden explosion from Mrs. Potts' back*

*yard. The women freeze in their positions. The noise
is exactly like gunfire.* FLO *speaks first in an ominous
voice*)

FLO   Helen!

MRS. POTTS (*Nervous*)   I'll go see what it is.

FLO   Stay here! He had a *gun*.

MRS. POTTS' MOTHER (*Off stage*)   Helen! Helen!

FLO (*Anxiously*)   Don't go back there, Helen. Your
mother's old. She has to go soon anyway.

ALAN (*Comes running on, tossing a package of chickens
onto porch*)   What happened?

FLO   Oh, thank heaven you're here, Alan. Helen Potts
took in some hoodlum with a gun.

ALAN   A gun?

FLO   Madge, you run upstairs and take care of that
dress. Alan's here now, Helen. He'll go with you.

MRS. POTTS (*Running off*)   Pshaw! I'm not afraid.
(ALAN *follows her a little way to make sure she's all
right.* MADGE *goes inside*)

ROSEMARY   I'm sure the young man had a gun. I'm
sure.

ALAN (*Seeing everything is all right*)   No one has a
gun. It's all right.
(*He is studying* HAL *in the distance*)

MRS. POTTS (*Coming back and facing* FLO)   I was a
bad girl.

FLO (*Still excited*)   What *is* it, Helen?

MRS. POTTS   I got a *new* bottle of cleaning fluid, and I
threw *it* into the trash this morning instead of the old
one.

FLO (*Fans herself*)   Oh!

MRS. POTTS   The young man's more frightened than we
were. He ran into my laundry line trying to get away.
Come help me, Millie.

MILLIE (*Following* MRS. POTTS *off*)   Sure!

MADGE (*Sticking her head out the window*)   Mom, can
you finish my dress now?

FLO (*Hurrying inside*)   All right! All right!
(ROSEMARY *joins* ALAN *in peering off at* HAL. ALAN
looks at her and she becomes self-conscious)

ROSEMARY   I hope no one got hurt.
(*She takes herself inside. Now* ALAN *recognizes* HAL.
Obviously his feelings are mixed. He calls)

ALAN   Hal! Hal! Come on over.

HAL (*Before coming on*)   Hi'ya, Al!

ALAN   You've given the ladies quite a shock.

HAL (*Comes on, putting on a T-shirt. There is soot on
his face and body*)   Well, I always do *that,* Al.
(ALAN *isn't prepared to be amused*)

ALAN (*Straight to the point*)   What're you doing *here?*

HAL   Aren't you even gonna say hello?

ALAN (*In one word*)   Hello!

HAL (*Realizing all is not well*)   Oh! (*Innocently*) I
didn't figure I was stealin' your car, Al.

ALAN   What name did *you* invent for it?

HAL   Well, I knew you had insurance. Right?

ALAN (*Belligerent*)   Of course!

HAL   So I knew you'd get yourself a *new* car without
putting out any dough. I even figured I might be doin'

you a favor, helpin' you to get a new car. (ALAN *shrugs his shoulders hopelessly.* HAL *continues urgently*) And I *had* to get to California, Al. I just *had* to. Once I got out there, I was tellin' myself, I'd soon be able to pay you back. Yah! I'd pay you back double.

ALAN You mean . . . once you crashed the movies!

HAL (*A little embarrassed*) Well . . . other guys have done it, Al.

ALAN Did you finally get out?

HAL Yah, I got out.

ALAN *How?*

HAL After I smashed your car, I went home. The old man died, Al.

ALAN Oh . . .
(*He's not ready yet to say he's sorry*)

HAL He left me a little insurance. I used that.

ALAN Did you get a test?

HAL Yah! I got the test okay.

ALAN That's more than I expected.

HAL I don't see why one of those talent scouts'd come to see me play football and tell me he'd get me a screen test . . . if he didn't mean it.

ALAN It happens at school every year.

HAL (*Reliving the experience enthusiastically*) I was about to have a big career, Al! Yah! They were gonna call me *Brush* Carter. How ya like that? They took a lotta pictures of me with my shirt off. Real rugged. Then they dressed me up like a pirate, like the Foreign Legion, then put me in a pair of tights and a cape, gave me a sword and a big hat with lots of plumes, and there I was . . . (*Pantomine*) makin' with the sword-play. You shoulda seen me, Al.

ALAN   Didn't they give you any lines to read?

HAL   Yah. That part went okay. It was my teeth.

ALAN   Your teeth?

HAL   Yah! You see, out there you gotta have a certain kind of teeth, or they can't use you. They told me, they'd have to pull all my teeth, for some reason, and gimme new ones. Yah!

ALAN   (*Coming to his own conclusion*)   Oh!

HAL   This babe explained the whole thing to me.

ALAN   *What* babe?

HAL   The babe that finally got me the test.

ALAN   (*Putting two and two together*)   Oh!

HAL   Well . . . I was just *nice* to her. That's all. Anything wrong with *that?*

ALAN   (*Suddenly*)   Let's get to the point, Hal. You're *broke*. You've come all the way back here to . . .

HAL   I hitchhiked, Al.

ALAN   . . . to borrow money off me because you figured I'd be a big enough sap to give it to you.

HAL   Gee, Al, I don't see why you have to put everything in black and white like that.

ALAN   I can't help you, Hal.

HAL   All I want is a *job*.

ALAN   Look Hal, I'm *out* of college now. I'm beginning to settle down, and . . .

HAL   I'm a good worker, Al.

ALAN   Maybe you are!

HAL   I was on a ranch *all* summer, Al. Out in Nevada. Workin' hard, too. In bed every night at ten, up at six. No liquor! No babes! You'd been proud of me, Al.

ALAN   Well . . .
      (*Not knowing what to do*)

HAL   Come across, Al. Give a guy a break.

ALAN   I'm not Henry J. Kaiser. I don't have jobs at my fingertips that I can distribute to everyone who comes along.

HAL (*Abashed*)   Sure, Al!

ALAN (*Suddenly wanting an explanation*)   Why do you come to *me*, Hal? Always to *me!*

HAL (*Embarrassed*)   Cause . . .

ALAN   Tell me!

HAL (*A sad fact he hates to admit*)   You're the only friend I got, Al.

ALAN (*Resisting any appeal to his sympathy*)   Cut it!

HAL   It's a fact! You know how it was in the fraternity. All those other bastards always looking down their noses at me! Makin' sure I used a fork instead of a knife! You're the only decent guy I know in this whole fouled-up world.

ALAN (*A little dubious*)   Gee . . . thanks!

HAL   It's *true!* You're the only friend I got, whether you wanta be or not.

ALAN   Well, why don't you go *home?*

HAL   Not since the old man died. *Huh-uh!*

ALAN   Maybe your mother *needs* you.

HAL   *Needs* me? Not *her*. She's doin' O.K. She took over the old man's filling station. She's in the gravy.

ALAN   Then get a job from *her*.

HAL   (*Full of deep misgiving*)   I can't even look her in the face, Al . . . without gettin' *sick*.

ALAN   Hal, that's not fair to your own mother.

HAL   The old man left the filling station to *me* . . .

ALAN   Then go back and settle with your mother and . . .

HAL   But she told the lawyers he was bughouse, so *she* could take over.

ALAN (*Wincing*)   Oh! Golly!

HAL   See . . . the old man had started drinkin' again.

ALAN   Yah! You told me once he . . .

HAL   (*Obviously he loved his father*)   He'd been sober for six years. It looked like he was gonna stay that way. But the old lady had to have one more good fight out of him . . . So he went on his last bender.

ALAN (*Truthfully*)   Gee, Hal, I'm awfully sorry.

HAL   (*His face is set with determination. A few tears begin to well in his eyes. He grits his teeth and clenches his fists*)   It's the kinda thing that . . .
      (*He gropes for the words*)

ALAN   Easy, Hal!

HAL   I gotta *amount* to something, Al. I *gotta!*

ALAN (*Warm but reasonable*)   You're not going to do it overnight, Hal. You're not going to do it by playing football or trying to get in the movies.

HAL   Yah! I know.

ALAN   I'll get you a job, Hal.

HAL   That's all I want, Al. Just a job. A *good* job. I wanta be like *you*.

ALAN   Like *me?*

HAL   Yah, I'd like a job in a nice office, where I could wear a sharp suit, and give dictation to a secretary, and talk over the phone about . . . *enter*prises, and things.

ALAN   Look, Hal, I'm not much more than an errand boy, taking orders from everyone at the bank. I earn two hundred dollars a month.

HAL   Is that all?

ALAN   I know Dad has plans for me, but right now I'm content to stay here and *learn* the business, from the bottom up.

HAL   (*Thinking*)   It makes sense.

ALAN   If you wanta get somewhere, Hal, you just have to work hard and be *patient*.

HAL   (*Taking it all in*)   Yah! That's something I gotta learn . . . *patience!*

MRS. POTTS   (*Comes on carrying a lucious cake*)   Millie iced the cake for me.
    (MILLIE *follows with gooey frosting around her lips.* HAL *wipes the remaining wetness from his eyes, to remove any signs that he has been crying*)

HAL   Want me to run the vacuum for you, ma'am?

MRS. POTTS   No, Mama's sleeping now. You can just forget it. I feel I've been more than paid for the breakfast.

HAL   S'pose there's any place I could wash up?

MRS. POTTS   Oh dear! If you used my bathroom now, you'd wake Mama . . .

MILLIE   We got a shower in the basement.

MRS. POTTS   Would Flo mind, Millie?

MILLIE (*To* HAL)   Come on. I'll show you.
   (HAL *follows* MILLIE *inside,* MILLIE *is now carrying the cake*)

ALAN   Sinclair is hiring lots of new men, aren't they?

MRS. POTTS   Yes, Alan! Betsy Hamilton told me Carey wanted a hundred new men to put in the new pipeline.

ALAN   Yah! I hear they're paying good salaries, too.

MRS. POTTS   Oh yes! Those men make very good money now. They're all driving new cars.

ALAN   I'll call Carey Hamilton this afternoon.

ROSEMARY (*Coming out in a new outfit which she wears with arrogant defiance. A trim suit, a small fur piece, and a most elaborate hat*)   Is this a private party I'm crashing?

MRS. POTTS (*Awed by* ROSEMARY'S *splendor*)   My, you're dressed up!

ROSEMARY   'S my new fall outfit. Got it in Kansas City. Paid twenty-two fifty for the hat.

MRS. POTTS   You school teachers do have nice things.

ROSEMARY   And don't have to ask anybody when we wanta get 'em, either.

FLO (*Coming out,* MADGE *following*)   Be here for lunch today, Rosemary?

ROSEMARY   No. There's a welcome-home party down
at the hotel. Lunch and bridge, for the *new* girls on the
faculty. Irma Kronkite's coming by for me.

MADGE   Mom, can't I go swimming, too?

FLO   Who'll fix *lunch?* I've got a million things to do.

MADGE   It wouldn't kill Millie if she ever did any cook-
ing.

FLO   No, but it'd kill the rest of us.
(Now we hear the voices of IRMA KRONKITE *and*
CHRISTINE SCHOENWALDER *who are coming by for*
ROSEMARY. *They think it playful to call from a dis-
tance)*

VOICES   Rosemary! Rosemary! Let's get going, girl!
Hurry up, Rosemary! We don't wanta be late.
(Now they come on. IRMA *is past forty but keeps her-
self trim.* CHRISTINE *may be younger and more naïve.
Both are dressed in the best their budgets can provide,
So they appear, if not chic, undeniably well dressed.
On any social occasion, they are as boisterous as Girl
Scouts)*

IRMA   *(To Christine, when they come on)*   You'll *love*
Rosemary Sydney. She's a peck of fun. Says the
craziest things!

ROSEMARY   *(Calling out, with playful suspiciousness)*
What're you saying about me, Irma Kronkite?
*(Now they see each other and run to clasp each other
in their arms, like eager sisters who had not met in a
decade)*

IRMA   Rosemary Sydney!

ROSEMARY   Irma Kronkite!

IRMA   Kid, it's good to see you back. How was your vacation?

ROSEMARY   Slept under blankets every night. How was yours?

IRMA   I worked like a slave. But I had fun, too. I don't care if I *never* get that masters. I'm not going to be a slave *all* my life.

CHRISTINE (*Shyly*)   She's been telling me about all the wicked times she had in New York, and *not* at Teachers College, if I may add.

IRMA   Kid, this is Christine Schoenwalder, taking Mabel Freemont's place in Feminine Hygiene.

ROSEMARY (*Offering a hand*)   We're gonna be great friends, Christine. I can tell.

CHRISTINE   I certainly hope so.

IRMA (*Calling up to the porch*)   Been a hot summer, Mrs. Owens?

FLO   Terrible! Good to see you back, girls.

MRS. POTTS   Welcome home, girls!
    (MADGE *and* MILLIE *exchange a "Hi!" with* IRMA)

IRMA (*To* ROSEMARY)   Kid, we better get a hustle on. (*They are about to start off*)

CHRISTINE   Tell her about Helen Hayes, Irma.

IRMA   Kid, I saw all the smash-hit shows in New York.

ROSEMARY   I love a good show.

IRMA   And I had this one friend took me backstage to meet her. She was *sweet!* Just as natural as you and I.

ROSEMARY   I hear the play isn't any good.

IRMA   No! there aren't any good plays any more.
(*The teachers go off.* FLO *seems observant of* ROSE-
MARY. MADGE *and* ALAN *talk together*)

FLO   I think Rosemary'd smother in those winter clothes.
I don't care *how* she denies it, she's out to get a man.

MRS. POTTS   But she's always talking about not having
any use for a man.

FLO   Talk's *cheap.*
(*Now* HAL *and* MILLIE *speed out the door, tossing a
beach ball between them*)

ALAN   Wanta go swimming, Hal? I've got extra trunks
in the car.

HAL   Why not?

FLO   (*Surprised that* HAL *has come out of her house*)
Why, when did he . . . ?

ALAN   (*Taking over*)   Mrs. Owen, this is my friend Hal
Carter. He's a fraternity brother.

FLO   (*She couldn't have dreamed it*)   *Fraternity!*

HAL   Glad to make your acquaintance, ma'am.

FLO   (*Flabbergasted*)   Well . . . any friend of Alan's
is a friend of ours.
(*Finally she comes through with a smile*)

HAL   Thanks, ma'am!

MRS. POTTS   Now Millie has a date for the picnic.

FLO   Yes! Mrs. Potts and I are having a picnic for the
young people. You come, too.

HAL   I don't think it's right, me bargin' in this way.

MRS. POTTS   (*Exuberant*)   Nonsense! A picnic's no fun
without lots and lots of young people. I'm going to
bake another cake.

(ALAN *had not counted on* HAL'S *going on the picnic.
He looks a little uncomfortable*)

HAL (HAL *and* MILLIE *toss the ball between them now,
right of doorstep*)   Isn't your sister goin' swimmin'?

MILLIE   No. Madge has to cook lunch.

HAL   Do you mean *she cooks?*

MILLIE   Oh! Madge cooks and sews and does all those
things that women do.
(*Still tossing the ball, they run off to the car together.*
ALAN *and* MADGE *are having a tête-à-tête as* FLO *inter-
rupts*)

FLO   Alan!

ALAN   Yes?

FLO   Is that boy really a fraternity brother?

ALAN   Hal? Oh! well . . . (*He is stumped*) Well, he's
not really a fraternity brother because he never was
initiated, but . . .

FLO   I don't see how a boy like him ever got to *college.*

ALAN (*Proudly*)   Oh! Hal made a spectacular football
record in high school, down in Arkansas. The coach
brought him to the campus and gave him his expenses
and tuition . . .

FLO   But why would your fraternity take him?

ALAN   A fraternity *likes* to pledge football players. It's
good publicity. Hal *starred* in every game of the season.

FLO   But why didn't they initiate him?

ALAN (*Slowly*)   Well . . . he broke an arm Thanks-
giving and the doctor told him he could never play
again.

MRS. POTTS   And your fraternity put him *out?*

ALAN   Well . . . the other fellows really didn't like Hal.

FLO   Of course they didn't.

MRS. POTTS   Why, I think those fraternities are the most snobbish institutions I ever heard of.

ALAN   Sometimes I blamed the fellows. Sometimes I had to blame Hal. I guess it's no one's fault really.

MADGE   Was he blackballed?

ALAN   That's the word they use.

FLO   (*The first time she ever encountered the word*) *Blackballed!*

ALAN   Mrs. Owens, now that we've asked him, I don't think we should worry.

FLO   Helen Potts, *you* asked him. Why don't you mind your own business?

MRS. POTTS   He'll be company for Millie.

ALAN   Everything'll be all right.

FLO   Is he *wild?*

ALAN   (*Avoiding it*)   Oh . . . not really . . . he just . . .

FLO   Of course he is! Does he drink?

ALAN   A little! (ALAN *is trying to minimize it*) Hal pays attention to *me,* Mrs. Owens. I'll see that he behaves.

FLO   I wouldn't want anything to happen to Millie.

MADGE   Mom, Millie's perfectly capable of looking after herself. You *pamper* her.

ALAN   (*Laughing it off*)   Oh! Hal and Millie will get on *great.*

MRS. POTTS   And we've already asked him, Flo.
   (FLO *looks worried*)

ALAN (*To* MADGE)   See you this evening, dear.

MADGE   About five thirty.
   (*They laugh and he kisses her. Then they drift arm in arm, away from the doorstep, as though they had private things to say*)

MRS. POTTS (*To* FLO)   I was just thinking. Wouldn't it be nice if Alan were more like the young man, and the young man were more like Alan?

FLO   A woman can't expect a man to be everything.

MRS. POTTS   No. Of course not.
   (*Now there is a loud blast of the horn on* ALAN'S *car. Those on stage jump a little and look out at* HAL, *making the disturbance*)

HAL   Hey, Al! Get the lead outa your pants.
   (*Obviously annoyed,* ALAN *leaves* MADGE *and goes to the car.* FLO *looks daggers out at* HAL. *The blasting of the horn continues until the curtain comes down*)

Curtain

Act Two

*It is late afternoon, the same day. The sun is be-
ginning to set and fills the atmosphere with radiant orange. When the curtain goes up,* MILLIE *is on the stage
alone. She has permitted herself to "dress up" and wears
a becoming, feminine dress in which she can not help
feeling a little strange. Nevertheless, she also seems to be a
little pleased with herself. She has put on a little make-up
and is quite attractive. Dance music issues from the radio,
kept on the porch during the summer, and* MILLIE *ca-
vorts over the porch with an imaginary partner, waltzing,
swirling, tangoing, or at least giving her own untutored
versions of same. For the first time one is aware of her
repressed girlishness. Finally* MADGE *comes onto the
porch, dressed as she was in Act One.* MADGE *is still
begrudging the fact that she had to get the picnic supper
ready without any help from* MILLIE.

MADGE   I don't know why you couldn't have helped us
in the kitchen.

MILLIE   (*Lightly, giving her own version of the sophisti-
cated belle*)   I had to dress for the ball.

MADGE   I had to make the potato salad, and stuff the
eggs, and make three dozen bread and butter sand-
wiches. I feel like an old kitchen slavey.

39

MILLIE (*In a very affected accent*)   I had to *bathe* . . . and dust my limbs with powder . . . and slip into my frock . . .

MADGE   Did you clean the bathtub?

MILLIE   Yes, I cleaned the bathtub.

MADGE   It's a wonder.

MILLIE (*Shyly now, daring to ask the question*)   Madge?

MADGE   What?

MILLIE   How do I look? Tell me the truth.

MADGE   You look all right.

MILLIE (*Having hoped for a little more*)   Do I, Madge?

MADGE   I guess so.

MILLIE   I feel sorta funny.

MADGE   The dress is pretty.

MILLIE   It was *yours*. Do *I* ever get any new dresses? No. "Here's an old dress of Madge's. It'll do for Millie." (*Serious again*) Madge!

MADGE   What?

MILLIE   How do you talk to boys?

MADGE   Why, you just talk, silly.

MILLIE   But how d'ya think of things to say?

MADGE   I don't know. I guess you just say the things that come into your head.

MILLIE   But nothing ever comes into my head.

MADGE   Talk to boys the same as you'd talk to anyone else.

MILLIE   Somehow . . . it's different. (*Another long pause*) Madge?

MADGE What?

MILLIE Do you think Hal's good lookin'?

MADGE (*If she does, she's not letting anyone know it*)
Maybe . . . in a sort of way.

MILLIE I think he's a big show-off. You should have
seen him this afternoon at the swimming pool. He got
up on the high diving board and did real graceful swan
dives, and a two and a half gainer, and a back flip . . .
and all the girls stood around clapping. He ate it up.

MADGE (*Her mind elsewhere*) I think I'll paint my toenails tonight and wear sandals.

MILLIE And he was bragging all afternoon. He said he
used to be a deep-sea diver off Catalina Island.

MADGE Honest?

MILLIE And he says he used to make hundreds of dollars doing parachute jumps out of a balloon. Do you
believe it?

MADGE I don't see why not.

MILLIE You never hear Alan bragging that way.

MADGE Alan never jumped out of a balloon.

MILLIE Madge, I think he's girl crazy, too.

MADGE You think every boy you see is something horrible.

MILLIE Alan took us into the Hi Ho for Cokes and
there was a gang of girls in the back booth. Juanita
Badger and her gang. When they saw him, they
started giggling and tee-heeing and saying all sorts of
crazy things. Then Juanita Badger comes up to me
and whispers, "He's the cutest thing I ever saw." Is he,
Madge?

MADGE   I certainly wouldn't say he was "the cutest thing I ever saw."

MILLIE   Juanita Badger's an old floozy. She sits in the back row at the movie so the boys that come in will see her and sit with her. One time she and Rubberneck Krauss were asked by the management to leave. And they weren't just kissin' either.

MADGE (*With a feeling of superiority*)   I never speak to Juanita Badger.

MILLIE (*Approaching the real question she has been leading up to*)   Madge?

MADGE   What is it?

MILLIE   Do you . . . think he'll like me?

MADGE   I don't know.

MILLIE   I . . . I just wonder.

FLO (*Comes out onto the porch, having finished in the kitchen*)   I tell myself I got two beautiful daughters now.

MILLIE (*Embarrassed*)   Be quiet, Mom.

FLO   Doesn't Millie look pretty, Madge?

MADGE   I guess so.

MILLIE (*To* FLO)   You're just saying that because you're my mom.

FLO   Does that keep it from being true?

MILLIE   People we love are always pretty.

FLO   Well?

MILLIE   People who are pretty to begin with, then everybody loves them.

FLO   Well, now everybody will love *you*. Run over and show Helen Potts how pretty you are.

MILLIE   (*Running off in a wild parody of herself*)   Here comes Millie Owens, the great beauty of all time! Be prepared to swoon when you see her!

FLO   (*Very intimately to Madge*)   I wish you'd give the child more encouragement.

MADGE   (*In a sullen mood*)   Why?

FLO   Millie needs confidence.

MADGE   *Millie?*

FLO   Yes.

MADGE   That's all I hear, is *poor* Millie. And she made the highest grades in the whole junior class last year. She won herself a scholarship for four whole years at college. And she writes stories and draws pictures that everyone is always giving her compliments about, and all I hear is poor Millie.

FLO   A woman can need confidence in other ways.

MADGE   How do you mean?

FLO   I guess you wouldn't understand.

MADGE   I guess I'm too dumb to understand. Is that what you mean?

FLO   No! You're just not old enough or experienced enough. (*Studies* MADGE *a moment*) I want you to look after Millie tonight.

MADGE   Why?

FLO   I'm sorry we ever asked that young hooligan to take her on the picnic.

MADGE   Hal?

FLO   Yes, Hal, or whatever his name is. There's something about him I don't like.

MADGE   He's just an ordinary boy. Just 'cause his folks don't have a lot of money, is that anything against him?

FLO   He left every towel in the bathroom black as dirt.

MADGE   What's so horrible about that?

FLO (*Very privately*)   He left the seat up, too.

MADGE   It's not going to hurt anyone to be nice to him.

FLO   Just the same, you look after Millie. I want her to get interested in some boy, but not some young hoodlum like this . . . this *Hal*. And if there's any drinking tonight, you put a stop to it.

MADGE   I'm not going to be a wet blanket.

FLO   If the boys feel they have to have a few drinks, I guess there's nothing you can do about it, but you can keep Millie from taking any.

MADGE   I can't keep Millie from doing anything if she takes a notion to do it.

FLO   You can set her an example by not taking any yourself.

MADGE   Why are you so worried about Millie?

FLO   She's a moody child. She'll get in trouble enough in her own good time, without any assistance from strangers.

MADGE (*After a long pause*)   Mom!

FLO   Yes?

MADGE   What good is it to be pretty?

FLO   What a question!

MADGE   I'm serious.

FLO Well . . .
(*Apparently she is formulating her thoughts on the matter*)

MADGE Is that all it means, just standing around for people to *tell* you how pretty you are?

FLO Well . . . pretty things are rare in this life.

MADGE But what *good* are they?

FLO Pretty things like sunsets . . . and flowers . . . and rubies . . . and pretty girls, too . . . they're like billboards telling us life is good.

MADGE (*Beginning to reconsider*) Oh!

FLO Living can be hard and folks can get pretty discouraged, but when we see something beautiful it all seems worth while.

MADGE That's just fine, but where do I come in?

FLO What do you mean?

MADGE Maybe I get tired of being looked at.

FLO Madge!

MADGE Well, maybe I do!

FLO Don't talk so selfish.

MADGE I don't care if I *am* selfish. It's no good just being pretty. It's no good.

FLO A woman's life . . . whether she's pretty or not . . . never means anything to *her* till it means something to someone else.

MADGE (*Thinks a moment but unsuccessfully*) I don't get it.

FLO Maybe you never will. Go get dressed.

MADGE (*Getting up, looking into the distance*) Here comes Rosemary and the other old maids.

FLO Don't talk so disrespectful. You may be an old maid yourself some day.

MADGE (*Proudly going into the house*) I bet I'm not.

FLO (*Calling out to the teachers*) Good evening, girls! (ROSEMARY, IRMA *and* CHRISTINE *come on together, their arms entwined*)

IRMA We've brought home your wayward girl, Mrs. Owens.
(*The teachers stop before the house to have a final bit of gossip*)

ROSEMARY Say! You could have knocked me over with a feather when I heard that Myrtle Jefferson got married.

IRMA Me, too, girl.

CHRISTINE I knew Myrtle at State Teachers. There used to be all sorts of stories about her.

IRMA Mary Lou McCord came up to me just before we sat down and introduced the new girl taking her place. It must have been very sudden.

ROSEMARY You remember how she complained last spring about not feeling well.

IRMA You're thinking the same thing I am.

ROSEMARY I never mentioned it before, but I used to hear my students talking about her all last year.

IRMA About her and that Brooks boy?

ROSEMARY Yes. One of her own students.

IRMA Kid, I don't approve of things like that.

ROSEMARY Neither do I!

IRMA (*Suddenly full of Christian generosity*) Well, I'm not going to say any more. All I hope is that Myrtle is happy. I say that in all honesty.

ROSEMARY Oh, I never had anything *against* Myrtle.

IRMA (*About to start off*) We'll come by for you in the morning, Rosemary.

CHRISTINE (*Grabs* ROSEMARY'S *hand warmly*) Kid, I'm so happy to have met you. You know something? I feel we're old friends already.

ROSEMARY I feel the very same way.
(IRMA *and* CHRISTINE *go off, their heads together in resumed chit-chat.* ROSEMARY *drags herself up on the porch, wearily*)

FLO How was the party?

ROSEMARY Wasn't a real party. Each girl paid for her own lunch. Then we played bridge all afternoon. Lord, I get tired playing bridge.

FLO Have anything good to eat?

ROSEMARY I had a French-fried pork chop and it was mostly fat. Linda Sue Breckenridge—she's the sewing teacher—she had pot roast of veal and there was only one little hunk of meat in it. All we girls made Linda Sue call the waiter and complain.

FLO Food isn't very good at the hotel, but they serve it to you nice.

ROSEMARY Yes, they always have clean tablecloths and honest to goodness napkins. Lord, I hate paper napkins.

FLO What time's Howard coming by?

ROSEMARY Said he'd be here to take me to dinner.

FLO   You're welcome to go on the picnic with us.

ROSEMARY   I don't think so. There's always so many ants.

MADGE   (*Coming back out*)   Miss Sydney, could I use some of your Shalimar?

ROSEMARY   I guess so.

FLO   Why are you primping extra for tonight, Madge?

MADGE   I'm *not*.
(*She sounds a little too definite*)

FLO   Don't you have nice perfume of your own?

MADGE   I want a change.
(*She goes haughtily inside*)

ROSEMARY   (*Sagely*)   Madge thinks too much about boys, Mrs. Owens.

FLO   Madge?

ROSEMARY   I don't think there's anything *wrong* with Madge. Don't misunderstand. But when she was in my shorthand class, I noticed things.

FLO (*Defensively*)   Like what?

ROSEMARY   Boys always notice Madge, of course, and Madge . . . Well, most of the time, Madge noticed the boys, too.

FLO   Well, Madge is *normal*. She's at an age when she notices . . . things.

ROSEMARY   Madge pretends to be mighty independent, but she likes boys. I think you oughta watch her.

FLO   Why Madge has never gone out with any boy but Alan.

ROSEMARY   I'm not saying there's anything *wrong* with Madge. Don't misunderstand.

(FLO *is huffy, but the argument is stopped by the excited entrance of* MRS. POTTS, *dragging* MILLIE *by the arm. Each of them carries a cake*)

MRS. POTTS   It's a *miracle!* That's what it is, a miracle! I never knew Millie could look so pretty. It's just like a movie I saw once. Betty Grable was in it . . . (*Thinks a moment*) Or was it Lana Turner . . . Anyway, whoever it was, played the part of a secretary to some very important businessman. She wore glasses and did her hair real plain, and men didn't pay any attention to her at all. Then one day she took off her glasses and she was the prettiest thing you ever saw. Her boss wanted to marry her right away. That's what I tell Millie. All the boys are going to fall in love with her.

ROSEMARY   I always did say, if Millie took a little pride in her appearance, she'd be prettier than Madge.

FLO (*Finally getting back*)   Rosemary, you just don't like Madge. Admit it!

ROSEMARY (*Shocked*)   Why, Mrs. Owens! Why shouldn't I like Madge? It just so happens that, whereas other people are always raving about how beautiful Madge is, I just never happened to think so. That's all.

MRS. POTTS   Oh, Madge is the prettiest girl in town.

ROSEMARY   Does Millie have a date tonight?

FLO   Yes. The young man over at Helen's this morning . . . turned out to be a friend of Alan.

ROSEMARY (*She remembers*)   Oh . . . him!

MRS. POTTS   Yes, and he's a very nice young man. I'm sure of it.

FLO   Millie, take the cakes to the kitchen.

MRS. POTTS (*Handing her the one she has been holding*)
One's a Lady Baltimore. The other's an orange-co-
coanut layer.

ROSEMARY (*Jumping up from her chair*)   It's him! It's
him!
(HOWARD'S *Chevrolet is heard chugging to a stop*)

MRS. POTTS (*Turning to see*)   Who? Oh, it's Howard.
(*Waves blithely*) Hello, Howard!

ROSEMARY (*Sitting back down*)   If he's been drinking,
I'm not going out with him.

MRS. POTTS   He looks all right to me, Rosemary.

HOWARD (*Before coming on*)   Howdy, ladies! (*Now,
in the upstairs window,* MADGE *can be seen starting to
get dressed. From now until her appearance on stage,
her dressing is a sort of ritual expressing the fondness
with which she regards herself. Having come from the
bath, she dusts herself with powder, slips into her lingerie, and studies herself at the mirror while she ap-
plies her make-up. When* HOWARD *comes up the walk,
he sees her but doesn't permit himself to linger.*
HOWARD *is a small, thin man around forty. His face is
lined and filled with uncertainty but he maintains always a cheerful disposition. He is neatly dressed and
quite sober. He comes up onto the porch*) You sure
look nice, Rosemary.

ROSEMARY (*Her tone of voice must tell a man she is independent of him*)   Seems t'me you mighta left your
coat on.

HOWARD   Still too darn hot, even if it is September.

FLO   How are things over in Cherryvale, Howard?

HOWARD   Good business. Back to school and everybody buying.

ROSEMARY   When business is good, it's good for everyone.

MRS. POTTS   Maybe Howard would like a piece of my cake, Rosemary.

HOWARD   That's a good idea. I didn't get any lunch today.

ROSEMARY   It'll spoil your supper.

HOWARD   We'll call this *tea,* like the English people do. Every day 'bout this time, they have tea. It's a regular meal with them.

FLO   Helen Potts makes the best Lady Baltimore in town.

ROSEMARY   (*With repressed animosity*)   People *say* Mrs. Potts' cakes are very good.

MRS. POTTS   You talk like you never had a piece. I always bring my cakes over here.

ROSEMARY   You always seem to, when Howard's here. (*She goes haughtily inside*)

MRS. POTTS   Now I wonder if I made her mad.

HOWARD   Rosemary can get mighty uppety.

FLO   She gets over it.

MILLIE (*Coming out*)   Hi, Howard!

HOWARD   Hello, Millie-my-girl! What you dressed up for?

MRS. POTTS (*With enthusiasm*)   Millie has a *date.*

HOWARD   Well, I'll be darned. (*Announced as his own discovery*) Millie's not a bad-looking kid.

MRS. POTTS I tell her, all the boys are going to fall madly in love.

MILLIE Mom!

FLO What is it?

MILLIE What time did they say they'd be here?

FLO At five thirty. You've asked me a dozen times.
(*Obviously* MILLIE *is restless. She wanders about the porch, not knowing precisely what to do with herself*)

ROSEMARY (*Coming out with a piece of cake on a plate*) Here's your cake, Howard. I brought you a fork to eat it with, so don't use your fingers.

HOWARD Thanks, Rosemary.

ROSEMARY Howard, Mrs. Owens wants us to go on the picnic.

FLO There's plenty of food.

MRS. POTTS Oh, *do* come!

ROSEMARY I think it might be fun.

HOWARD Whatever you say, honey.

ROSEMARY (*Seems jovial*) Good! We'll all go on the picnic together.

MILLIE (*Privately to* FLO) Mom, I feel scared.

FLO Why?

MILLIE 'Cause he's a boy.

FLO You'll get over it.
(*Sounds are heard of two automobiles, one with a very powerful motor*)

MILLIE Mom, here they are. I don't wanta go.

FLO (*Too absorbed by the arrival to notice* MILLIE) Alan's brought *both* cars. Imagine being rich enough to have two cars.

MRS. POTTS (*Nudging* FLO) Some day *you'll* be riding around in that big Cadillac. Will you be too high-hat to call on your old neighbor?

ROSEMARY Is that your boy friend, Millie, driving the Ford?

MRS. POTTS Isn't he handsome?

ROSEMARY I never pay any attention to handsome men.

MILLIE (*Wanting to bolt*) I'll go inside and tell Madge they're here.

FLO (*Dragging* MILLIE *back by the arm*) Madge can take care of herself. Stay here.

MRS. POTTS Goodness, yes, Millie. You've got a boy friend coming to call. Stay and greet him.

ROSEMARY I think the picnic's going to be loads of fun, Howard.
(*Since the automobiles were first heard, all eyes have been directed off stage at the boys*)

ALAN (*Before coming on*) Everyone ready?

FLO Come on up, Alan.

ROSEMARY (*Very stimulated by their arrival, compelled to act as hostess*) The more the merrier!

ALAN (*Coming up*) I brought both cars. We can put the baskets in the Ford. Dad's always so careful about the upholstery in the Cadillac.

ROSEMARY (*Nudging* HOWARD) I've always wanted to ride in Alan's Cadillac.

ALAN (*Calling back to* HAL, *who has been held a moment by the vision of* MADGE *in her window*)   Come on, Hal!

HAL   I sure didn't mean to keep anyone waiting.

FLO (*To* ALAN)   Madge'll be down soon.

ALAN   You've met Mrs. Potts, Hal.

HAL (*Putting an arm around her*)   Oh, she's my best girl.

MRS. POTTS (*Beaming*)   You're just joking.

HAL (*Expansively, as though making an announcement*) This little lady took pity on me when I was starving. Some character on the train robbed me of every cent I had. I usually travel with plenty of money, too.
(*The women are very aware of him but seem to wonder what to make of him*)

ALAN   And this is Rosemary Sydney, Hal. Miss Sydney teaches shorthand and typing in our high school.

ROSEMARY (*Steps up with a wide grin and a proffered hand*)   Yes, I'm an old-maid school teacher.

HAL (*Very earnestly*)   I have every respect for school teachers, ma'am. It's a lotta hard work and not much pay.
(ROSEMARY *cannot decide whether the remark is a compliment*)

ALAN (*About to relax*)   It's certainly been a hot day, hasn't it? (*But he has overlooked* HOWARD *whom he finds now tugging at his elbow*) Oh, I'm sorry. Hal, this is Howard Bevans, from Cherryvale. Mr. Bevans is a friend of Miss Sydney.

HAL (*Shaking hands*)   Very honored to make your acquaintance, Mr. Bevans.

HOWARD   You a friend of Seymour's?

HAL   Oh, Al and I are buddies.

HOWARD   I run a little shop over in Cherryvale. Notions, novelties, school supplies. Bring Alan over some time and get acquainted.

HAL (*Again, very earnest*)   Sir, I'll speak to Alan about that tomorrow. We'll come over as soon as we can fit it into our schedule.

FLO (*Privately to Alan*)   Alan, has your friend been drinking?

ALAN   Oh, just a few beers, Mrs. Owens.

FLO   I thought so.

ALAN   But he isn't tight. He'll be all right, I promise.

HAL (MILLIE, *all this time, has been waiting*)   Hi ya, Millie! Say, you got a little more tan, didn't you? *You* look great.

MILLIE (*Meekly*)   Thanks.

HAL (*Another general announcement*)   You folks should have seen Millie this afternoon. She did a fine jackknife off the high board. And I wouldn't admit this to many people, but she does a jackknife that's almost as good as mine. See, I used to be diving champion on the West Coast. I know what I'm talking about.

MRS. POTTS   Oh, Millie's a very talented girl.

HAL   When I got in town this morning, I sure didn't realize I'd find a good-lookin' kid like Millie waitin' for me.

MILLIE (*Smiling and blushing*)   Cut it out.
(HAL *and* MILLIE *seem to be getting along, he acting like a big brother*)

HAL   What's the matter, kid? Think I'm snowin' you under?

FLO (*Privately*)   I think things are going to work out all right, Alan.

ALAN   Like I said, Hal is fine, if you just give him a chance.

ROSEMARY (*Has been looking at the boots somewhat fascinatedly*)   Where'd you get those boots?

HAL (*Still addressing the company*)   I guess maybe I should apologize for the way I look. But you see, that character on the train, he made off with all my clothes, too. Yah! I had several suitcases full of very fine tailored suits.

MRS. POTTS   What a pity!

HAL (*With a hopeful, ingenuous laugh*)   I just didn't want you folks to think you were associatin' with a bum. Ha! Ha!

MRS. POTTS   Clothes don't make the man.

HAL   That's what I tell myself, ma'am.

FLO   Is your mother taken care of, Helen?

MRS. POTTS   Yes, Flo. I've got a baby-sitter for her. (*General laughter*)

FLO   Then let's get the baskets ready.

HAL (*Continuing his explanation to* ROSEMARY)   See, ma'am, my old man left me these boots when he died.

ROSEMARY   That all he left ya, just a pair a boots?

HAL   He said, "Son, the man of the house needs a pair
a boots 'cause he's gotta do a lotta kickin'.
"Your wages all are spent,
The landlord wants his rent.
You go home to your woman for solace,
And she fills ya fulla tor*ment*."
That's a little poem he made up. He allus said, "Son,
there'll be times when the only thing you got to be
proud of is the fact you're a man. So wear your boots
so people can hear you comin', and keep your fists
doubled up so they'll know ya mean business when
ya get there." (*He laughs*) My old man, he was a
corker!

HOWARD   What line of business you in, son?

HAL   (*Expands with importance*)   I'm about to enter the
oil business, sir.

HOWARD   Oh!

HAL   Ya see, my father was a very aristocratic million-
aire once, before he lost it all, and he had some very
important friends who were going to help me. One of
them wanted me to take a very high position with this
oil company, but . . .

ALAN   (*Matter-of-factly*)   Dad and I have found a place
for Hal on the pipeline.

HAL   (*Deflated*)   Gee, Al, I think you oughta let *me*
tell the story.

ALAN   Sorry, Hal.

HAL   (*For all who will listen*)   You see, I've decided
to start in from the very bottom, 'cause that way, I
think a guy learns things lots better. I'm gonna learn
all about the oil business the hard way, 'cause I think

I'll be happier in the end, even if I don't make much money for a while.

MRS. POTTS   Money isn't everything.

HAL   That's what I told myself, ma'am. Money isn't everything. There's lots of things in this life more important than money. I guess I've learned that much. All I ask for the present is a job that I can settle down with and start looking toward the future. And I certainly do appreciate Alan and his old . . . father giving me this chance.

HOWARD   It's a good business town. A young man can go far.

HAL   Yes, sir, I intend to go far.

HOWARD   He's gotta work hard.

HAL   I know that, sir. And I'm a hard worker. I know I'm going to have success one of these days. The only thing that worries me . . .

HOWARD   What's that?

HAL   (*Very earnestly*)   I don't want my success to come . . . before I'm *ready* for it.

HOWARD   (*Trying to digest it*)   Yes.

HAL   That's why I'm startin' in at the bottom.

MRS. POTTS   I think that's wonderful.

FLO   Come on, Helen.
     (*But* MRS. POTTS *doesn't hear*)

ROSEMARY   A young fellow, just coming to town, he's gotta be a good mixer.

HOWARD   Be a good plan for you to join the Young Businessmen's Club, meet every Tuesday for lunch at the hotel. I come over sometimes from Cherryvale.

MRS. POTTS   Wouldn't it be nice if he could join the Country Club?

ROSEMARY   I bet he'd like the bowling team, Howard. (*To* HAL) It's a rowdy gang.

MRS. POTTS   And there's a young men's Bible Class at the Baptist Church.

HAL   Oh, I plan to join clubs and go to church and do all those things.

FLO   (*Getting a little impatient*)   Helen, let's get the baskets ready.

MRS. POTTS   Oh, yes, Flo!

FLO   Alan, we'll need a man to help us.

ALAN   Right with you, Mrs. Owens.

MILLIE   Mom, do you need me?

FLO   No, Millie.

HAL   What's the matter, kid? You tryin' t'get away from me?
(*He laughs, treating Millie with bearlike affection*)

FLO   Come on, Helen.
(MRS. POTTS *would stay forever, but she follows* FLO *and* ALAN *into the house*)

HAL   (*Sitting, on the doorstep, he leans back, stretches onto the porch and gives in to dreamy reflection. All seems well in his life at the moment, and he can safely phantasize the future*)   You know, there comes a time in every man's life, when he's gotta settle down. I guess I've kicked around long enough. A little town like this, this is the place to settle down in, where life is quiet and easygoin', and people are . . . well, people are sincere.

(*This has amounted to little more than a monologue to which the others have paid little attention.* MILLIE *sits by his side.* ROSEMARY *and* HOWARD *are having a tête-à-tête*)

ROSEMARY (*Unheard by* HAL *and* MILLIE)   No, Howard, I don't think there oughta be any drinking if Millie's here.

HAL (*Deciding it's time to start a conversation*)   What have you been doin' with yourself all day, Millie?

MILLIE   I read a book.

HAL (*Impressed*)   You did?

MILLIE   Yes.

HAL   You mean, you read a whole book, in one day?

MILLIE   Yes.

HAL   I'll be damned. Was it good?

MILLIE   *I* thought so.

HAL   What was it about? Tell me.

MILLIE   Well . . . it's kinda hard to tell about.

HAL   What was the story?

MILLIE   There wasn't much story. It was all about these people . . .

HAL   Yah?

MILLIE (*Struggling to convey her impressions of the book*)   Well . . . they were interesting. That's all. And it made you feel kinda warm inside to read about them, and they were funny, too, and sad . . .

HAL (*Another phantasy coming on*)   You know, I wish I had more time to read. That's what I'm gonna do when I settle down. I'm gonna read all the better books, and listen to all the better music, like symphonies. A man owes it to himself. (MILLIE *just looks at him*) I used to go with a girl who read books. She joined the Book-of-the-Month Club and they had her readin' books all the time. She wouldn't any more finish one than they'd send her another.

ROSEMARY (*Still with* HOWARD) There'll be more food tonight than you can shake a stick at. Those women have been cookin' all day.

HOWARD (*Starting toward his car*) I say we need a little appetizer.

ROSEMARY Howard, where you goin'?

HOWARD I'll be right back, honey.
(*He disappears*)

ROSEMARY Howard, leave that bottle right where it is.

HAL (*Jumping*) Did she say "bottle"?

ROSEMARY (*Turning to* HAL) He's been down to the hotel, buyin' bootleg whiskey off those good-for-nothin' porters.

HOWARD (*Coming back with a fifth of whiskey*) Young man, maybe you'd like a swig of this.

HAL Hot damn!

HOWARD Millie's not gonna be shocked if she sees someone take a drink, are you, Millie?

MILLIE Gosh no!

ROSEMARY What if someone'd come by and tell the school board? I'd lose my job quick as you can say Jack Robinson.

HOWARD   Who's gonna see you, honey? Everyone in
town's out at the park, havin' a picnic.
(*Gives bottle to* HAL)

ROSEMARY   I don't care. Liquor's against the law in this
state, and a person oughta abide by the law. (*To* HAL
for confirmation) Isn't that what you say, young fellow?

HAL   (*Who must always agree*)   Oh, sure. A man's
gotta abide by the law.
(*But he takes a hearty swig nonetheless*)

HOWARD   A fellow's gotta have a little drink once in a
while, law or *no* law. Isn't that what *you* say, young
fellow?

HAL   (*With no awareness of contradiction*)   Oh, sure,
he's gotta.

HOWARD   Here, honey, have one.

ROSEMARY   No, Howard. Put that away.

HOWARD   Come on.

ROSEMARY   No, Howard, I'm not gonna touch a drop.

HOWARD   One isn't gonna hurt you.

ROSEMARY   I said *no,* and I *mean* no.

HOWARD   (*Giving it all the appeal of which he is capable*)
Come on, honey, have one little drink just for *me.*

ROSEMARY   (*Beginning to melt*)   Howard, you oughta
be ashamed of yourself.

HOWARD   (*With all innocence*)   I don't see why.

ROSEMARY   I guess I know why you want me to take a
drink.

HOWARD   (*Deeply offended*)   Now, honey, that's not so.
I just think you should have a good time like the rest

of us. (*To* HAL) School teachers gotta right t'live. Isn't that what you say, young fellow?

HAL (*Generously*)   Sure, school teachers gotta right t'live.

ROSEMARY   Now, Millie, don't you tell any of the kids at school.

MILLIE (*Sore*)   What do you take me for?

ROSEMARY   Anyone coming?

HOWARD   Coast is clear.

ROSEMARY (*Finishing a hearty drink out of the bottle*) Whew! I want some water.

HOWARD   Millie, why don't you run in the house and get us some?

ROSEMARY   Lord no, Howard, Mrs. Owens'd know what we wanted it for. I'll get a drink out of the hydrant. (*Goes to the side of the house, drinking from her cupped hands. Now there comes from the park the plaintive sound of a cowboy band that features a vibrant guitar. They play melodies like "Hey, Good Lookin'," "San," "I'm Dreaming Tonight of Your Blue Eyes," "Everybody Loves My Baby," all in easy, Western swing*)

HOWARD (*To* HAL)   Young man, have a drink now to celebrate your new job.

HAL   Sure!

HOWARD   It's not a very lively part of the country, but a person learns to like it.

HAL   I'm not hard to please.

HOWARD   Millie-my-girl, I'd like to offer you one, but I s'pose your old lady'd raise Ned. (*Toasts* HAL) Here's to what ails you. (*They drink, then* HOWARD *draws* HAL *to one side and nods at* MADGE'S *window*) You know, every time I come over here, I look forward just to seein' her.

HAL (*With all impartiality*)   Oh, she's a very nice-looking young lady.

HOWARD   I tell myself, "Bevans, old boy, you can look at that all you want but you couldn't touch it with a ten-foot pole."

HAL   Yah?

HOWARD   Anyway, I like to look at her. They tell me every boy in town has been on the make for that since she was old enough to go to Sunday school. Your friend Seymour, he's been off to school and picked up a little class; I guess she's pretty impressed. But Seymour, he don't know what it's *for*.

HAL   Al, he's a very serious young man.

HOWARD   The other boys, they come smellin' around once in a while, but from what I hear, they're gettin' pretty discouraged. I guess Seymour's *got* her.

HAL   Al, he'll make a fine husband.

HOWARD   You know, sometimes it breaks a fellow's heart to think a pretty girl like her ever gets old. Seems t'me, when the good Lord made a girl pretty as she is, He did it for a reason, and she oughta find out what that reason is before she settles down with some jerk, don't properly appreciate her. (*Nudges* HAL) You know what I mean.

HAL (*Loyal to the end*)   Oh, she and Al, they get along fine. She's nuts about Al.

HOWARD (*With another plaintive look at her window*) Anyway, I still like to look at her.

HAL   Yah! She's awful pretty.

HOWARD   Look, son, if you're agonizin', I know a couple of girls down at the hotel. I haven't seen 'em in quite a while, but they'll remember me if you give 'em my name. Just tell the porter you wanta see *Babs* . . . or Caroline . . . (*Thinks a moment and gives a little laugh*) Or both . . . you're a *young* fellow.

HAL (*Devoutly*)   I've given up that sorta thing.

HOWARD   Yah?

HAL   There comes a time in every man's life when he's gotta think about . . . well, more serious things.

HOWARD (*Solemnly*)   I think that's a fine attitude.

ROSEMARY (*Returning from the hydrant*)   What're you two talking about?

HOWARD   Talkin' about the weather, honey. Talkin' about the weather.

ROSEMARY   I bet. (*The whiskey has begun to show its effect. She sways rapturously to the music*) Lord, I like that music. Come dance with me, Howard.

HOWARD   Honey, I'm no good at dancin'.

ROSEMARY   That's just what you menfolks tell yourselves to get out of it. Well, I'll show you. (*Turns to* MILLIE, *alone on the doorstep*) Come dance with me, Millie.

MILLIE   I gotta lead.
   (ROSEMARY *and* MILLIE *dance together in a trim, automatic way that keeps time to the music but little else. Both women seem to show a little arrogance, in dancing together, as though boasting to the men of their independence. Their rhythm is accurate but uninspired.* HOWARD *and* HAL *watch, laughing*)

HOWARD   S'posin' Hal and I did that.

ROSEMARY   Go ahead for all I care. (HOWARD *turns to* HAL *and, laughing, they start dancing together,* HAL *giving his own clown's version of being the coy female. Then* ROSEMARY *and* MILLIE *stop and watch them.* ROSEMARY, *for some reason, becomes outraged*) Stop it!

HOWARD   I thought we were doin' very nicely.

ROSEMARY   It makes me sick to watch.

HOWARD   It was all right for you and Millie.

ROSEMARY   That's different.

HAL   Come on and dance with me, Millie.

MILLIE   (*Uncertain*)   Well . . . I never danced with boys.

HAL   Honest? (MILLIE *shakes her head, no*) You gotta try sometime.

MILLIE   I don't know how to follow.

HAL (*Very gently*)   Just relax, and do the steps *I* do.

MILLIE   I always want to do the steps I make up, my-self.

HAL (*Taking her in his arms*)   Come on and try.
    (*They dance together, but* MILLIE *has an awkward feeling of uncertainty which shows in her dancing*)

ROSEMARY   Quit clowning, Howard, and dance with me.

HOWARD   Honey, you don't get any fun out of dancing with me.

ROSEMARY   The band's playin'. You gotta dance with someone.
    (*They dance, doing a sort of uncertain toddle*)

HAL   Just relax, Millie.

MILLIE   I . . . I can't.
(*But they continue trying*)

ROSEMARY (*Her eyes closed in hard-sought ecstasy*)
Lord, I love to dance. At school, kids all called me
the Dancin' Fool. Went somewhere dancin' every night.

MRS. POTTS (*Appears in the doorway*)   I can't stay in
the kitchen while there's dancing.
(*She is like a child at a circus*)

HAL (*Stops the dancing intermittently to deliver needed
instructions to* MILLIE)   Now look, kid. You gotta
remember *I'm* the man, and you gotta do the steps
I do.

MILLIE (*Earnestly*)   I'll try.
(*They start off again*)

MRS. POTTS   Just relax, Millie.

MILLIE   I'm doing the best I can.

HAL   No one's complainin', kid.

ROSEMARY (*Continuing her reverie*)   One night I went
dancin' at a big Valentine party. I danced so hard I
swooned. That's right, I swooned, right in the center
of the dance floor. That's when they called me the
Dancin' Fool.

HAL (*A little impatient but still fraternal*)   Look, kid,
you just don't get the idea. I'm the leader. *I* make up
the steps we do. Just relax and follow *me*.

MRS. POTTS   Try again, Millie. Try again.

MILLIE (*Beginning to get flustered*)   Well . . . (*They
try again and* MILLIE *stumbles*) I'm sorry.

HAL   That's all right, kid. Don't let it get you down.
Rome wasn't built in a day.

MILLIE (*After stumbling again*)   I'm awfully sorry.

HAL   Forget it.

MILLIE   I . . . I don't want to . . . any more.
(MILLIE *withdraws to a corner of the porch to nurse
her feeling of incompetence*)

MRS. POTTS   Don't give up, Millie. Keep trying. (*But
MILLIE can't be drawn back out of her corner. By now
HAL is too far gone with the music to pay attention
to any but his own feelings. The music now is keeping
a happy rhythm and HAL does a few steps of his own,
not elaborate or very catchy steps, but rhythmic. MRS.
POTTS hurries to MILLIE'S side*) Go back and dance
with the young man, Millie. The young man wants
someone to dance with. Go back and try.
(MILLIE *just withdraws further, turning her back on
the scene. Then MADGE comes out the front door,
looking very beautiful in her new dress and very happy
to be confronted by dancing*)

MADGE   Is everyone dancing?

HAL   Hi!
(*Here is the person to complete HAL'S rhythm. He
takes her immediately in his arms, MADGE quite willing
to be taken, and they dance together as one. HAL is a
good dancer and MADGE is fluid line in his arms. They
do a well-modulated jitterbug and, when he swings her
body free from his own, it is remarkable to see how
their bodies still respond to each other even at a distance. Now MRS. POTTS is drawn from MILLIE to
watch HAL and MADGE, whose dancing delights her*)

MRS. POTTS   Oh, I *love* to watch people dancing.
(*Then ROSEMARY and HOWARD give up their own
movements to watch*)

ROSEMARY   Come look, Howard.
(HAL *and* MADGE *dance with more intense rhythm*)

MRS. POTTS   They dance like they were made for each
other, don't they?

ROSEMARY   Howard, can't *you* dance that way?

HOWARD   Me?

ROSEMARY   That's the way t'dance, Howard. *That's* the
way.

HOWARD   Honey, if I danced that way, all my customers'd think I was unreliable.

ROSEMARY   Lord, I love to dance.
(*Now the music comes to a temporary end and* MADGE
and HAL *break apart*)

MADGE   Alan always says it's all right for me to dance
with other boys.

MRS. POTTS (*Applauding*)   Dance some more. *Please*
dance some more.

ROSEMARY (*Having decided to make her own bid for*
HAL)   Dance with *me,* young man. Dance with me.
(*She places herself in his arms*)

HAL   Well, ma'am, I . . .

ROSEMARY   I may be an old-maid school teacher, but
I can keep up with you.
(HAL *can do nothing but give in to her. She clamps her
arms about his neck, shoving her hips hungrily up to
his loins, keeping her cheek plastered against his own*)

MRS. POTTS (*Running back inside the house*)   Oh, I
love to watch people dance. I love to watch people
dance.
(*By this time,* HOWARD, *with a sheepish grin, has
moved in on* MADGE *and gained her consent for a*

dance. MILLIE *has never felt more utterly alone. She finds the whiskey bottle and makes her first experiment.* ROSEMARY, *with* HAL, *continues her running monologue*)

ROSEMARY   I used to have a boy friend was a cowboy. Name was Hoot. Met him in Colorado when I went out there t'get over a case of flu. He was a *dashing* young fellow. He was in love with me . . . 'cause I was an older woman and had some sense. Took me up in the mountains one night and wanted me to marry him, right there on the mountain top . . . said God'd be the preacher, the moon our best man. Ever hear such talk?

HAL (*Weary*)   Ma'am, I'd like another li'l drink.
(MILLIE *has been sipping at intervals, but now the bottle is back on the porch*)

ROSEMARY   Howard, where's that bottle? It's time *we* had a turn. (*She brings the bottle to* HAL *after taking a swig herself. She is becoming bawdy*) Lord, I like those boots.

HAL (*Innocently*)   Yah?

ROSEMARY   A man looks like more of a man with boots on.

HAL (*Getting embarrassed*)   Yah . . . well . . .

ROSEMARY   You know what happened at school last year? We had a statue of one of those Roman gladiators in the library. All he had on was a pair a boots and helmet. Oh, those ancient people were depraved. Harriet Bristol got up a petition among all the teachers, and the principal agreed. So the school janitor took a chisel, one afternoon when school was out, and he got busy and made that gladiator decent.

HAL (*A little sickened*)   Ma'am, I don't think I feel like dancing.

ROSEMARY   Whatsa matter?

HAL   I guess maybe I'm kinda tired.

ROSEMARY   A big man like you? With those broad shoulders and those big arms? You're not tired.

HAL (*Not wishing to offend*)   Ma'am . . . I guess I just don't feel like dancing any more.

ROSEMARY (*Burns for a moment*)   Oh! You don't *wanta* dance with *me!*

HAL   No offense, ma'am.

ROSEMARY   I guess *I'm* supposed to feel *insulted.*
    (*She begins dancing by herself, executing a series of wild, high kicks*)

HOWARD   Now, how'd my bottle get over here?
    (*He finds his bottle where* MILLIE *left it*)

ROSEMARY (*Pivoting around the stage, doing one high kick after another*)   At school, I was the Dancin' Fool. I danced so hard one night, I *swooned.* That's right. I swooned right in the center of the ballroom.
    (HAL *and* MADGE *stand quietly together, as though cautiously becoming aware of each other*)

MADGE   I have a T.L. for *you.*

HAL   Honest?

MADGE   Mrs. Potts thinks you're one of the nicest boys she ever met. She says you're a Prince Charming look-ing for his kingdom. That's what she said.

HAL   Gee, it's nice to hear something like that.

MADGE   Now, tell me mine. And compliments from Alan don't count.

HAL   Well, Howard's been talkin' all evening about how pretty you are.

MADGE   Oh, Howard's nice.

HAL   He says you're the prettiest girl in town.

MADGE   I don't really think so. But that's why I was voted Queen Neewollah.

HAL   Was it?

MADGE   Every year they have a big Halloween celebration, and there's a big coronation ceremony at the Memorial Hall, with artistic singing and dancing. Every town in the county sends a queen, but I was queen of them all. I had to sit through the whole ceremony until they put the crown on my head. The *Kansas City Star* had pictures in their Sunday rotogravure. Most people expected me to get real conceited, but I didn't.

HAL (*Gullible*)   You didn't?

MADGE   I don't like people who are conceited, do you?

HAL   Naw!

ROSEMARY (*Still dancing*)   I did the Charleston and the Black Bottom and all those wild dances.
(*She executes another fairly successful high kick*)

HOWARD (*A quiet spectator, his bottle beside him*) Rosemary's got pretty legs, hasn't she?

ROSEMARY (*Howard has provided her with a new opportunity to make a spectacle. His quiet remark brings forth from her an eruption of harsh laughter*)   That's just like you men, can't talk about anything but women's legs.

HOWARD   That's not so, honey. You kicked your leg in the air, and I just noticed that it had a good shape.

ROSEMARY   I don't care. That's all you men talk about,
is women's legs. How would you men folks like it if
we women went around talkin' about *your* legs all the
time?

HOWARD   (*Ready to be a sport, jumps up and lifts his
trousers to his knees*)   All right, there's *my* legs. Go
ahead and talk about 'em.

ROSEMARY   (*This is too much for her*)   Never saw anything so ugly! Men's big hairy legs with wads of muscle
in 'em. Never saw anything so ugly.
(*She laughs and slaps her thighs*)

HOWARD   (*Dropping his trousers*)   All right, you don't
have to look at 'em, if you don't want to.

ROSEMARY   (*Now boldly invades the privacy of* HAL *and*
MADGE, *snatching* HAL *forward*)   Young man, let's
see your legs!

HAL   Huh?
(*He is unprepared for this new attack*)

ROSEMARY   We passed a new rule. Every man here's
gotta show his legs.

HAL   Ma'am, I got on boots.

HOWARD   (*Interceding*)   Rosemary, let him alone. He
wants to be with Madge. They're *young* people.

ROSEMARY   (*In a hollow voice*)   Young? Whata you
mean, they're *young?*

MILLIE   (*Suddenly running forward, gripping her stomach*)   Oh, I'm sick.

MADGE   Millie!

MILLIE   I wanta die.

HOWARD   What'd the li'l dickens do, get herself tight?

HAL   Take it easy, kid.

ROSEMARY (*Groping blindly across stage, suffering from* HOWARD'S *remark*)   I suppose that's something wonderful. They're *young*.

MADGE   Let's go inside, Millie.

MILLIE   Get away from me.

HOWARD   Mrs. Owens is gonna raise Ned.

MADGE   Come on, Millie. I just wanta help.

MILLIE (*With angry tears*)   Don't touch me. I hate you.

MADGE (*Hurt*)   Millie!

MILLIE   Madge is the pretty one! Madge is the pretty one! Madge is the pretty one!
(*She runs inside crying, holding the sickness in her stomach. She leaves behind her a long, embarrassed silence*)

MADGE (*Finally*)   Mom is gonna kill me.

ROSEMARY (*Confronting* HAL)   Young man, this is all *your* fault.

HAL   Huh?

ROSEMARY   *Millie* was your date, not Madge. Madge, you should be ashamed of yourself.

MADGE   I don't see why.

ROSEMARY   You come out here on the front porch, wearing your new dress, wearing my expensive perfume stuck behind your ears, and take him right out of Millie's arms. I saw you. Don't deny it.

MADGE   Millie didn't want to dance.

ROSEMARY (*To* HAL)   There's just too many worthless young men like you, runnin' loose over the country today. No jobs, no responsibilities, spongin' off decent, self-respecting people, tryin' to make yourself at home where you're not wanted.

HAL (*Dumfounded*)   Gee!

HOWARD   Rosemary, take it easy. He's not done anything.

ROSEMARY   I know what I'm doin', Howard. Oh yes, you come stompin' around here in your boots like you owned the place . . .

HAL (*Amazed*)   Huh?

ROSEMARY   Showin' decent ladies the hair on your chest, struttin' around like someone's prize rooster, thinkin' every woman you saw was gonna fall madly in love . . .

HOWARD   Rosemary, soft-pedal it.

ROSEMARY   But here's *one* woman that didn't pay you any mind. I saw through you right from the start. (*Mocking*) My father, he was a very wealthy man. A very wealthy friend of his was gonna give me a very high position with his firm, but I wanta start in at the bottom. (*Hal gulps. He winces with the pain of recognition*) It's all a pack of lies. You never had a pot.

HOWARD (*Shocked*)   Rosemary!

ROSEMARY   Be quiet, Howard. (*Continuing*) I'm gonna read all the *better* books and listen to symphonies. I'll bet you couldn't recite the alphabet, and you couldn't tell music from thunder.

HOWARD   Rosemary, what's got into you?

ROSEMARY (*By this time she is in a frenzy of emotion*) And you'll never amount to a hill of beans because you're no good, and a person can tell that just by

lookin' at you. You're nothin' but Arkansas white
trash, and you'll end your life in a gutter.

HOWARD (*Jumps over to* ROSEMARY, *clamps a hand over
her mouth*)   Rosemary, shut your God damn mouth.
(*But her words had their effect on* HAL. *He has
crumpled on the doorstep, his face in his hands, trying
to hold his insult and rage*)

FLO (*Flying out onto the porch like a hornet*)   What's
been going on out here? Who fed whiskey to my
Millie?

ROSEMARY   It was . . .

HOWARD (*Clamps a hand over* ROSEMARY'S *mouth again
and answers for her*)   Mrs. Owens, I'm mighty sorry.
I had a bottle of whiskey, and we were cuttin' up, not
payin' attention to what was goin' on, and Millie took
a few snifters without anyone knowing.

MADGE   That's right, Mom. She did it just to be mean.

MRS. POTTS (*Sticking her head out the door*)   Millie's
all right now, Flo. Alan held her head and let her
vomit. She feels perfectly all right. Now come along,
Flo.

FLO (*With an insinuating look at* HAL)   I certainly don't
like the looks of things.

MADGE   None of us saw her do it, Mom.

FLO   And I hope it's understood, there's to be no more
whiskey drinking on this picnic tonight. Is that clearly
understood by all?

MRS. POTTS (*Ushering* MILLIE *and* ALAN *out the door*)
Here's Millie now. And we're all going to start on the
picnic and forget it.

FLO   Are you all right, Millie?

MILLIE   Yes, I'm all right.

FLO   (*Rather high-handed*)   Millie will come with *us,* Alan.

ALAN   All right, Mrs. Owens. Come on, Hal. Let's put the baskets in the Ford.
(ALAN *goes off carrying a basket and a jug, leaving another basket on the porch.* HAL *hasn't moved from his place of despair.* MADGE *is the only one aware of his feelings. She hovers near him*)

FLO   (*Her arm around* MILLIE *as they start for the car.* MRS. POTTS *beside them*)   Come on, Helen.

MRS. POTTS   Why is it more fun to fix your supper at home and take it out to the park and eat it, than it is to stay home and eat it? It's the change. We all like a change. And if we had to go on a picnic every night, we'd be so tired of picnics we could die.
(FLO, MRS. POTTS, *and* MILLIE *go off*)

HOWARD   He's just a boy, Rosemary. You talked awful.

ROSEMARY (*Blankly*)   Did I, Howard?

HOWARD   You gotta remember, men have got feelings, too. Same as women.

ROSEMARY   I don't wanta go on the picnic, Howard. This is my last night of vacation and I wanta have a good time.

HOWARD   We'll go for a ride, honey.

ROSEMARY   (*Pointing into the distance*)   Look at that sunset, Howard.

HOWARD   Ya know, if ya painted that in a picture, no one'd believe it.

ROSEMARY I wanta drive into the sunset, Howard! I wanta drive into the sunset!
(*She goes running off to* HOWARD'S *car,* HOWARD *following.* ALAN *now returns*)

ALAN Come on, Hal!

HAL I'm not goin'.

ALAN What do you mean you're not going?

HAL Just what I say, I'm not goin'.

ALAN Hal!

HAL I wasn't doin' a God damn thing, I tell you. Mindin' my own business. Then suddenly I start gettin' hell for no reason at all.

MADGE Miss Sydney said some awfully mean things, Alan.

ALAN You've got to drive the Ford out. All the baskets are in the Ford.

HAL Oh, I've got to drive the Ford out, do I? I guess I'm a lousy servant. Well, if you think I'm gonna take any more crap like that you're crazy.

ALAN Hal, I've been pretty patient with you.

HAL Patient?

ALAN Yes, patient. In the fraternity, I was the only fellow that ever stood by you. Right?

HAL (*Softly*) Right.

ALAN I got you out of one mess after another. I got you reinstated by the Dean, I got you out of jail one morning, I got you off the blacklist at the Kappa House . . .

HAL (*Squirming with discomfort*) Jesus, Al, cut it out. Don't you think I got feelings?

ALAN   It wasn't *my* idea to ask you tonight. And I told you not to drink. But now we've got to make the best of it. So come along.

MADGE (*Sweetly to* HAL)   Come on, won't you?

HAL   (*Considering* MADGE'S *invitation, then to* ALAN) How'm I gonna find my way out there?

ALAN   Well . . . it's not far. You can follow me.

HAL   I gotta pick up the ice cream and get the tires filled.

ALAN   I'd forgot.

MADGE   Alan, I'll go with him and show him the way.

HAL   (*To* MADGE)   You don't understand, miss. Al don't think I'm good enough to 'ssociate with you fine people.

ALAN   (*Embarrassed*)   Hal, I never said that.

HAL   But you thought it, Al. You thought maybe if a solid citizen like you took a kindly interest in a bum like me, you could chalk one up for charity.

ALAN   (*Truly hurt*)   Hal!

HAL   Go on. I'll get your ice cream and find my way out there somehow. Then you can eat your fried chicken and all go take a flyin' fling at the moon, for all I care. I'll be hitchin' a ride outa town.

MADGE   Let me go with him, Alan.

ALAN   (*Distrustfully*)   Madge, I . . .

HAL   Seymour, he don't trust me. He don't trust anyone.

ALAN   Hal, that's not so.

MADGE   I think I *should,* Alan.

ALAN   Well . . . O.K. (*Trying to bring about a recon-
ciliation*) Madge will go with you, Hal. That O.K?
(HAL *prefers to be noncommittal.* ALAN *turns to*
MADGE)   See you later, dear. Goodbye!
(*He kisses her quickly on the cheek, then departs*)

MADGE   (*To* HAL)   You know what? I think you have
an inferiority complex.

HAL   Quiet, doll.

MADGE   (*Gives a little giggle*)   No one ever called me
"doll" before.

HAL   Yah?

MADGE   Honest!

HAL   Well . . . there's a first time for everything.

MADGE   We better go.

HAL   Come here, doll!

MADGE   We've got the basket with the fried chicken.

HAL   (*Appraising her from head to toe*)   Haven't we
just!

MADGE   They'll be waiting.

HAL   Look, baby. I got a hot news flash.

MADGE   What?

HAL   (*Suddenly and impulsively, he takes her in his arms
and kisses her devouringly*)   We're not goin' on no
God damn picnic.

Curtain

Act Three

It is very early the next morning. The sun is just be-ginning to rise and, in the atmosphere, there is that un-certain quiet that precedes total day. The stage is de-serted. After a few moments, the motor of HOWARD'S *Chevrolet is heard chugging to a stop at the side of the house. Then he and* ROSEMARY *come straggling on to-gether.* ROSEMARY *is densely preoccupied. She stumbles on almost blindly and drops to the doorstep.* HOWARD *is sleepy. He yawns.*

HOWARD (*After stretching*)   Here we are, honey. Right back where we started from.

ROSEMARY (*Her mind somewhere else*)   Uhh.

HOWARD   Honey, what're you gonna tell Mrs. Owens?

ROSEMARY (*A blankness in her eyes*)   I don't know.

HOWARD   She knows I got an aunt in the country. Why don'tcha tell her we go to my aunt's place? She would-n't think anything of that.

ROSEMARY (*She hasn't heard a word*)   Uhh.

HOWARD   A businessman has to think of those things, Rosemary.

ROSEMARY   Uh.

81

HOWARD (*Looking at his watch*)   Well, I just got time to have breakfast, then head back for Cherryvale in time to get the store open. Good night, Rosemary. I guess I should say, good morning!
(*He gives her a peck on the cheek, then starts off*)

ROSEMARY (*Just coming to*)   Where you goin', Howard?

HOWARD   Honey, I gotta get home.

ROSEMARY   You can't go off without me.

HOWARD   Honey, talk sense.

ROSEMARY   You can't go off without me. That's sense.

HOWARD (*A little nervous*)   Honey, be reasonable.

ROSEMARY   Take me with you.

HOWARD   What'd people say?

ROSEMARY (*Almost vicious*)   To *hell* with what people'd say!

HOWARD (*Shocked*)   Honey!

ROSEMARY   What'd people say if I thumbed my nose at them? What'd people say if I walked down the street and showed 'em my pink panties? What do I care what people say?

HOWARD   Honey, you're not yourself.

ROSEMARY   Yes, I am. I'm more myself than I ever was. Take me with you, Howard. If you don't, I don't know what I'll do with myself. I mean it.

HOWARD   Now look, honey, you can still go upstairs and get a little rest before school starts. Then I'll be back Saturday and we can talk all this over . . .

ROSEMARY   Maybe you won't be back Saturday. Maybe you won't be back ever again.

HOWARD   Rosemary, you know better than that.

ROSEMARY   Then what's the next thing in store for me?
To be nice to the next man, then the next . . . till
there's no one left to care whether I'm nice to him or
not. Till I'm ready for the grave and don't have anyone to take me there.

HOWARD (*In an attempt to be consoling*)   Now, Rosemary!

ROSEMARY   You can't let that happen to me, Howard.
I won't let you.

HOWARD   I don't understand. When we first started going together, you were the best sport I ever saw, always
good for a laugh.

ROSEMARY   I can't laugh any more.

HOWARD   We'll talk it over Saturday.

ROSEMARY   We'll talk it over *now*.

HOWARD (*Squirming*)   Well . . . honey . . . I . . .

ROSEMARY   You said you were gonna marry me, Howard. You said when I get back from my vacation, you'd
be waitin' with the preacher.

HOWARD   Honey, I've had an awful busy summer
and . . .

ROSEMARY   Where's the preacher, Howard? Where is he?

HOWARD (*Walking away from her*)   Honey, I'm forty-
two years old. A person forms certain ways of livin',
then one day it's too late to change.

ROSEMARY (*Grabbing him by the arm and yanking him
back to her*)   Come back here, Howard. I'm no
spring chicken either. Maybe I'm a little older than
you think *I* am. I've formed my ways, too. But they

can be changed. They *gotta* be changed. It's no good livin' like this, in rented rooms, meetin' a bunch of old maids for supper every night, then comin' back home alone.

HOWARD   *I* know it isn't, Rosemary. My life's no bed of roses either.

ROSEMARY   Then why don't you do something about it?

HOWARD   I figure . . . there's some bad things about every life.

ROSEMARY   There's too much bad about mine. Each year, I keep tellin' myself it's the last, something'll happen. Then nothing ever does . . . except I get a little crazier all the time.

HOWARD (*Hopelessly*)   Well . . .

ROSEMARY   A well's a hole in the ground, Howard. Be careful you don't fall in.

HOWARD   I wasn't tryin' to be funny.

ROSEMARY   . . . And all this time you just been leadin' me on.

HOWARD (*Somewhat defensive*)   Rosemary, that's not so! I've not been leading you *on*.

ROSEMARY   I'd like to know what else you call it.

HOWARD   Well . . . can't we talk about it Saturday? I'm dead tired and I got a busy week ahead, and . . .

ROSEMARY (*She grips him by the arm and looks straight into his eyes*)   You gotta marry me, Howard.

HOWARD (*Squirming*)   . . . Well . . .

ROSEMARY   You might just as well go down and get the license now.

HOWARD   Office isn't open yet.

ROSEMARY   It will be, by the time you get your breakfast.

HOWARD   Sometimes you're unreasonable.

ROSEMARY   Go get the license, Howard. I'll be waitin'.
(HOWARD *thinks it over for several moments, rubbing his chin, looking terribly harried. Then he speaks with decision*)

HOWARD   No!

ROSEMARY   Howard!

HOWARD   I'm not gonna marry a woman that says . . . "You gotta marry me, Howard." That's all there is *to* it. I'm not gonna. (*There is silence.* ROSEMARY *weeps real tears*) If a woman wants me to marry her . . . she can at least say "please."

ROSEMARY   (*Beaten and humble*)   Please marry me, Howard.

HOWARD (*Thinking it over*)   Well . . .

ROSEMARY (*Desperate*)   Oh, God! Please marry me, Howard. *Please!*

HOWARD (*Rather matter-of-fact*)   Well . . . all right!

ROSEMARY (*Hugging him*)   Oh, Howard!
(*She sobs and sobs*)

HOWARD   When do you wanta do it?

ROSEMARY   Now, Howard. Now. Please! I don't wanta wait another day.

HOWARD   Gee!

ROSEMARY   Please, Howard! Please!

HOWARD   What'll you do about your job?

ROSEMARY   I'll call the superintendent. He can get Alvah
Jackson to take my classes till they get a new teacher.
(ROSEMARY *seems almost breathless*)

HOWARD   Well . . . I gotta call Fred Joyce and see if
he can take care of the store for a few days.

ROSEMARY   Call him, Howard! Call him!

HOWARD   And I'll have to get a substitute to speak for
me at the Kiwanis Club dinner tomorrow night.

ROSEMARY   Then get him, Howard.

HOWARD   All right.

ROSEMARY   I'll be all packed by the time you get back.

HOWARD   Now I want time for a nice leisurely breakfast.

ROSEMARY   Sure, Howard! Goodbye, Howard!

HOWARD (*On his way to the car*)   Bye!
(ROSEMARY *goes excitedly into the house. The sun is
brighter now. A rooster crows in the distance. The*
NEWSBOY *comes on, whistling light-heartedly, and
throws a paper on the porch, after much ogling for a
glimpse of* MADGE. *He is on his way off when* BEANO
*dashes up on the porch with two quarts of milk, which
he sets by the door.* BOMBER *strolls on leisurely behind*
BEANO, *carrying a large wire basket full of milk bottles
and empties. The* NEWSBOY *sees them and waits*)

BEANO (*Calls to the* NEWSBOY)   Hey, Romney! The
Bomber's got somethin' to tell you.
(*The* NEWSBOY *turns and waits*)

BOMBER   Hear about it, Romney?

NEWSBOY   Hear about what?

BEANO (*On the porch*)   Tell him, Bomber!

BOMBER (*Moving closer to the* NEWSBOY) Glamour-puss got what's comin' to her last night.

NEWSBOY You're kiddin'.

BOMBER You can ask my brother. He saw 'em. So did a flock of other guys. They was down by the river, under the bridge.

NEWSBOY No foolin'?

BEANO (*Coming down from the porch*) He tell you, Romney?

NEWSBOY (*In a moment's phantasy*) Gee, she's pretty as movie stars.

BOMBER I *knew* she liked guys. She always put on a lotta airs, but I knew she liked guys.

BEANO (*Momentarily inspired, he has taken a pair of apples out of the* NEWSBOY'S *canvas newspaper sack and put one in each of the two breast pockets of his work shirt. Then he places an index finger in the center of his head and does a foolish dance, letting the apples dangle like women's breasts*) Hey, lookey! I'm Madge! I'm Madge!

BOMBER (*Digging into his pocket*) Let's have some fun.
(*He brings out a piece of chalk, hurries to the door-step, where he begins to scrawl in big white letters on the upright section of the step facing the audience*)

BEANO Hey, don't write anything *bad*.

NEWSBOY (*To* BOMBER, *grinningly*) You crazy guy!

BOMBER (*Finishing the sign which now all the audience can see,* MADGE LIKES GUYS) Anything so bad about that?

NEWSBOY Hey, they'll be sore.

BOMBER   Who cares? She's been goin' around with her nose in the air long enough, tryin' to make out she's too good.

NEWSBOY (*Going off dreamily, folding his papers*)   Gee . . . she's pretty as movie stars.

BEANO (*Privately to* BOMBER)   Hey, tell me honest. Do girls like fellas . . . the same as fellas like girls?

BOMBER   Where've you *been,* junior?

BEANO   I know you *say* they do, but I always wondered.

BOMBER   Look, junior, girls can get *nuts* about a guy.

BEANO   I always thought the guy, he gets nuts about the girl but the girl she don't get nuts about anything, *really,* 'cept pretty dresses and goin' to movies.

BOMBER   What d'ya think pretty dresses are *for?*

BEANO   To make her look pretty.

BOMBER   And why does she wanta look pretty? (BEANO *has never considered this. He rubs his chin.* BOMBER *says sagely*) You gotta lot to learn, junior.
(*They go off. Now* FLO'S *frantic voice is heard from inside the house. She is chastising* MADGE. MADGE'S *replies, if any, are too subdued to be heard so there are long pauses between* FLO'S *attacks*)

FLO (*Almost a scream*)   What happened? (*Silence*) Where did you go? (*Silence*) I'm going to call Alan Seymour and tell him to get over here as fast as he can. (*Now* MADGE *flees to the front porch, where she falls face down on the swing, giving in to floods of tears and convulsive sobs. She wears a robe over her nightgown.* FLO *follows later, wearing a house dress*) I never saw you like this before. I think I should call the doctor.

MADGE (*Between muffled sobs*)   Let me alone!

FLO   So *that's* why you had to wear your new dress.

MADGE   Let me alone, I tell you.

FLO   And *that's* why you had to wear Rosemary's per-
fume. *That's* why.

MADGE   It is *not*.

FLO   Look at me, girl. (MADGE *keeps her face hidden*)
Look at me, I say. (FLO *takes* MADGE's *face in one
hand and forces her to look at her*) Where did you
and that hoodlum go?

MADGE   No place.

FLO   Why didn't you come to the picnic?

MADGE   'Cause.

FLO   Where were you until three o'clock this morning?

MADGE   Let me *alone,* I say!

FLO   The nerve of some men, to walk right in, make
themselves at home and start making love to a girl
they never saw before.

MADGE   You just don't like him.

FLO   That's the God's truth. Now tell me what happened.

MADGE (*With hopeless sobbing*)   It just happened. I
don't know.

FLO   Shame! (FLO *says the one word so disparagingly
that* MADGE *can only break out in new tears.* FLO *is
keenly observant of* MADGE's *neck, for some reason*)
What's that on your neck?

MADGE (*Feeling her neck*)   Where?

FLO (*Closely inspecting*) Teeth marks. Madge, who was biting you? (MADGE *can only give in to new tears*) Listen to me, girl. (MADGE *keeps her head in the cushions*) Listen to *me*. I got things to say. (MADGE *finally raises her head*) There's true love in this life . . . and there's something else, excitement and heart throbs and thrills. All of them vanish after a few years, maybe after a few days. Then you hate yourself for having been such a fool, to let yourself be tricked, to have given up your entire life and all the years that lie ahead . . . because one night . . . something happened that made the blood trickle up your spine . . . that made your heart beat like a gong inside a cavern . . . that made you feel all of a sudden . . . like you'd found the whole reason for being born.

MADGE He . . . he *needs* me.

FLO (*Cynically*) Yes, he needs you. He needs you to stay home and fry potatoes and wash his underwear while he's at the pool hall. He needs you to forgive him when he spends all his wages on booze. He needs you to lie to when other women call the house and want to know where he is.

MADGE (*Angry*) Don't . . . don't say things like that.

FLO Now listen to me, girl, and listen close. Alan will be here in a minute.

MADGE I don't wanta hurt Alan's feelings. Honest, I don't.

FLO You've already hurt his feelings but that can't be helped right now. The point is, he *loves* you, and he's going to forget about this, maybe tomorrow, maybe today. Make up some story. He'll believe you because he *wants* to believe you, and thank you for sparing him the truth.

MADGE   I couldn't lie to Alan.

FLO   Then keep your mouth shut, and let me do the talking.

MADGE   (*In complete confusion*)   I . . . I don't know what to do.

FLO   (*Jumping at the sound of* ALAN'S *car*)   Here's Alan now. Dry your eyes. Don't let him see you've been crying. (*Rushing to the doorstep to welcome* ALAN) Good morning, Alan!

ALAN   (*Hurrying on to take* MADGE *in his arms*)   Madge!

FLO   (*Contented now*)   You and Madge stay here and talk, Alan. I'll go in and fix your breakfast. You and Madge can have it together.
(*She goes inside*)

ALAN   (*Tender, sounding very reasonable*)   Don't cry, Madge.

MADGE   I . . . I can't seem to help it.

ALAN   Where's Hal now?

MADGE   He spent the night at Mrs. Potts'.

ALAN   (*Hurrying to the edge of the porch and calling*) Hal! Hal! Get on over here as fast as you can. (HAL'S *head appears out of* MRS. POTTS' *back door. There is a wondering expression on his face.* ALAN *repeats his call.* ALAN *means business*) I said to get on over here.

HAL   (*Coming over, with a vague feeling of guilt*)   Yah! (*He still wears the T-shirt and jeans but is now barefoot*)

ALAN   (*Bringing a bill out of his pocket*)   The morning train will be along in a few minutes, Hal. Here's ten dollars. I want you to be on it.

HAL   Now, take it easy, Al.

ALAN (*Forcing the money on him*)   Take the money.
    You'll need it. Because if you're not on that train, the
    local police are going to pick you up on the first charge
    I can think of.

HAL (*Shocked*)   Al! You're kiddin'.

ALAN   Like fun!
    (*Obviously* ALAN *is not kidding*)

HAL (*At a loss*)   Gee, I don't know what to say.

ALAN   There's no need to say *anything*. Just *go*.

HAL (*Very humble*)   I'm sorry.

ALAN   Don't even be sorry. Just *go*.

HAL (*Giving the money back*)   I . . . I don't need
    your money, Al.
    (*He sounds defeated*)

ALAN   I want you to . . .

HAL   I can hop a boxcar. I done it before. (*He dares to
    look at* MADGE) Hi, baby!

MADGE (*Softly, rather wistful*)   Hi!

ALAN   Madge and I are going to be married, Hal.

HAL (*Trying to sound matter-of-fact*)   Yah? (*He looks
    at* MADGE) That right, baby? (MADGE *nods yes*) On
    the level? (*She nods again.* HAL *is really defeated. He
    appears almost sickened*) Oh! (*Thinks a moment*)
    No one told me that. Honest, no one told me.

ALAN   Would it have made any difference?

HAL   You gotta gimme the benefit of the doubt.

ALAN   Well, we're telling you now.

HAL (*Turning his back to them, his hands in his pockets,
    starting off*)   O.K. I'm goin'.
    (*But he is taking his time.* MADGE *is suspenseful*)

ALAN   Let him go, Madge.

MADGE (*To* ALAN)   I gotta talk to him.

ALAN   I don't see why.

MADGE   There are things I have to say.

ALAN   Say them here.

MADGE   I . . . I can't.

ALAN (*A little curt*)   I see.

MADGE   I'm sorry . . . but they're things I gotta say
    alone. (*Sees that* ALAN *is wounded*) And if I didn't
    say them, I'd be sorry the rest of my life.

ALAN   O.K. (*He's taking it like a man*) Hal, come over
    here. (*Sheepishly,* HAL *rejoins them*) Madge wants
    to talk to you. I'll go in and have my breakfast. (*Grabs
    HAL by the shirtfront*) But Madge and I are going
    to be married. And when I get back out here, I
    wanta see you on your way to that train. And if
    you're not, you know what'll happen, don't you?

HAL   Yah.

ALAN   O.K. Talk over whatever it is you've *got* to talk
    over. (*To* MADGE) I'll tell your mother you're dressing.
    (*He goes inside. There is an awkward silence between*
    MADGE *and* HAL)

MADGE   We wouldn't be happy together.

HAL   I don't see why not.

MADGE   Things like that don't last.

HAL (*Sounding rather naïve*)   Don't they?

MADGE   You make love to lots of girls.

HAL   . . . A few.

MADGE   Just like you made love to me last night.

HAL   Not like last night, baby. Last night was . . . (*He gropes for a word*) inspired.

MADGE   I'm not so conceited as to think I'm so much different from the others.

HAL   You're a woman, baby, an honest-to-God woman. And there aren't many such creatures left.

MADGE (*Shyly*)   Silly!

HAL (*Hoping to reseduce her, he jumps impulsively to her side and tries to get her in his arms*)   Baby, let's go through with our plan. You throw some things in a bag and we can hitchhike to Tulsa. Yah, we can make it in a couple hours. Then I can get a job, and we'll get a furnished room somewhere, and there'll be just the two of us, all cozy together, and . . .

MADGE (*His appeal is powerful. It takes all her character to resist*)   No.

HAL (*Knows he's licked*)   O.K.

MADGE   I'm going to marry Alan.

HAL   I heard you the first time.

MADGE   So, I just want you to know that I haven't any hard feelings, that I . . . I like you and everything but . . . I honestly think you better go.

HAL (*Beginning to show some of his soul's despair*) Jesus, is this as far as it ever goes for me? Is it?

MADGE   Please . . . please go.

HAL   O.K. Whatever you say. (*He looks straight in her eyes*) Kiss me goodbye.

MADGE   I don't think so.

HAL   Why? It's only fair to kiss a guy goodbye.

MADGE   Just the same. I'm not going to.

HAL   Afraid?

MADGE   No. Of course I'm not afraid.

HAL   You're lyin'.

MADGE   I am *not*.

HAL   Then kiss me to prove it.

FLO (*Shooting out onto the porch like a comet*)   Young man, I think you'd be ashamed to show your face after what happened.
(ALAN *is right behind her*)

ALAN   Let's go, Hal.

HAL (*Circumstances are against him*)   The nice lady washed my socks. I'm goin' soon as they're dry.

FLO   That train will be at the depot in exactly twelve minutes, and if you know what's good for you, you'll be on it even if you have to go barefoot.
(HAL *is beginning to smart a little*)

MILLIE (*Sticking her head out the door*)   Mom, Miss Sydney's packing all her things.

FLO (*Jumping at this annoying interference*)   What?

MILLIE   She's leaving.

FLO (*Bustling back inside*)   She can't do this to me. Who'll I rent her room to? She and I are going to have an understanding.
(FLO *and* MILLIE *go back inside*)

MRS. POTTS (*Hurrying on with* HAL'S *socks and boots*)
Young man, here's your socks. I put them in the oven
to get them dry. I found some polish for your boots,
too. See? They shine like new.

HAL   Thanks, ma'am.

ALAN   Now you can go, Hal.

HAL (*Somewhat sullen*)   Yah, now I can go.
(HAL *sits on the ground and begins putting on his
socks and boots*)

MRS. POTTS   Is the young man going?

HAL   Yes'm. I'm goin'.

MRS. POTTS   I thought you were gonna stay here and
settle down.

HAL   No'm. I'm not gonna settle down.

MRS. POTTS   What a pity!

FLO (*Bursting out of the door*)   Young man, are you
still here?

HAL   Gimme time to get my boots on.

MRS. POTTS   Young man, I have a brother down in
Okmulgee. He hires men for the Embassy Oil Company. You can tell him I sent you.

HAL   Thanks, ma'am, but I'll go *way* beyond Okmulgee.
(*The train whistles in the distance*)

FLO   That train will be at the station in exactly eight
minutes.

MRS. POTTS   The station's only two blocks from here,
Flo.
(FLO *looks daggers at* MRS. POTTS)

HAL (*To* FLO)   Relax, lady.

FLO   And we don't ever expect to see you around here again. Is that clear?

HAL   (*Some of his native hostility is returning*)   Yes, lady. You'll never see me around here again. That's *clear*.

ALAN   You better hurry, Hal.

HAL   (*Standing, looking at* MADGE *with a final appeal*) Goodbye!
(*But it sounds tentative.* MADGE *is at an impasse. Now from off stage we hear the morning voices of* IRMA *and* CHRISTINE *on their way to take* ROSEMARY *to school with them*)

IRMA   (*In the giddiest spirits*)   Kid, did I tell you, I went to the Stork Club?

CHRISTINE   Girl, you *didn't!*

IRMA   Well, I *did!* See, there was this fellow in my Educational Statistics class. He was a *peck* of fun. Said the *craziest* things! He and I made a bet. The one that made the lowest grade on the final had to take the other one to the Stork Club. I lost.

CHRISTINE   What was it like, the Stork Club?

IRMA   Balloons all over the place! Balloons!

FLO   (*Wanting to get rid of the teachers*)   Rosemary's inside, girls. She's expecting you.

IRMA   Thank you, Mrs. Owens.

CHRISTINE   (*She and* IRMA *are on porch now*)   How do I look, girl?

IRMA   It's a smart outfit. Let me fix it in back.

CHRISTINE (*As* IRMA *begins to readjust the hem*)   I believe a teacher should wear her best clothes first day of
school. To give the students a good first impression.

HAL (*His eyes still on* MADGE)   I said goodbye, baby.
(MADGE *can't answer*)

FLO   Young man, that train will be at the station in exactly six minutes, and if you're not on it, I'm going to
call the police.

HAL   Go on and call 'em. I'm gonna say goodbye.
(*With colossal strides, he goes to* MADGE, *takes her
forcefully in his arms and kisses her*)

ALAN   Hal!
(ALAN *jumps to* MADGE'S *side, trying to protect her
from* HAL. HAL *ignores him.* IRMA *and* CHRISTINE *nudge
each other.* FLO *is beside herself.* HOWARD *comes on
and stands gaping.* MRS. POTTS *is thrilled*)

FLO   I'm going to call them now. I should have called
them the minute you set foot on our porch. I'll have
you put in jail where you belong.
(FLO *darts inside.* ALAN *delivers a blow at* HAL *that
proves ineffectual.* HAL *then takes a sock at* ALAN *that
sends him to the ground*)

HAL   I'm warning you, Al, I'm a strong man and I'm
mad. I'll beat hell out of you if you don't let me be.
(ALAN *sits on the ground, rubbing his jaw.* HAL *takes
MADGE back in his arms and kisses her again*) I'm a
poor bastard, baby. A guy's gotta *claim* the things in
life that're *his*. When you hear that train whistle and
know I'm on it, your sweet little heart's gonna be
busted. And maybe it'll serve you right, 'cause you
love me, God damn it! You love me, you love me,
you *love* me!

(*Now he lets go of* MADGE *and runs off to catch his train.* MADGE *drops in a heap crying uncontrollably. The spectators have never had such excitement.* FLO *comes out, annoyed to find* IRMA *and* CHRISTINE *still present*)

FLO   I told you to go inside, girls. This is no sideshow we're running. (IRMA *and* CHRISTINE, *insulted, go into the house*) Go on in, Howard. Rosemary's expecting you. (*Surveys the landscape as* HOWARD *follows* IRMA *and* CHRISTINE) Is he gone?

MRS. POTTS (*Looking in the direction* HAL *has gone, in a hollow voice*)   Yes, he's gone.

FLO   Madge, get inside. All the neighbors are on their porches watching.

MADGE   I don't care.

FLO   Madge isn't herself, Alan. Stay and talk with her.

MRS. POTTS   I just remembered. I owe the young man a dollar for cleaning the lawn. And he needs the money so badly.

FLO   Helen, let him be.

MRS. POTTS   Maybe I can catch him. (*Runs off waving a dollar bill, calling in a plaintive voice*) Young man! Oh, young man!

FLO   Stay with Madge, Alan, and talk with her.
(*She goes inside*)

MADGE (*At edge of stage, watching in the distance*) He's getting on the train.

MRS. POTTS (*In the distance*)   Young man, can't you come back?

MADGE   . . . I'll never see him again.

MRS. POTTS (*In the distance*) I've something here that's
yours. Can't you come back?
(*The train is heard chugging away*)

MADGE The train's gone. (*A silence*) I feel like everything inside me was going with it.

ALAN (*He has been suffering through this, sitting on the
doorstep, his head in his hands*) Please . . . Madge!

MADGE (*Turning back to* ALAN) I'm sorry, Alan.
(*This is an impasse.* MILLIE *sticks her head out the
door*)

MILLIE Hey, Howard and Rosemary are gettin' married.

ALAN (*Somewhat sardonic*) Good for Howard and
Rosemary!
(MADGE *realizes this is the end between them. She
runs inside the house crying.* MILLIE *looks on quizzically*)

MILLIE What's the matter with *her?*

ALAN (*Shrugging his shoulders*) Girls have always liked
Hal.

MILLIE Girls can be crazy.

ALAN Months after he'd left the fraternity, they still
called. "Is Hal there?" "Does anyone know where he's
gone?" Their voices always sounded so forlorn.

MILLIE (*Shyly*) Alan!

ALAN (*Rather fondly*) What is it, Millie?

MILLIE I've always liked *you,* Alan. Didn't you know
it?

ALAN (*Truthfully*) No, I never did.

MILLIE It's awfully hard to show someone you like
them, isn't it?

ALAN   I suppose so. I don't know why.

MILLIE   I'm never going to have anything to do with love. Not me.

ALAN   Wait until you get a little older before you say that, Millie.

MILLIE   I'm old enough already. There's Madge inside, crying her eyes out, feeling like two cents. Do you think I'd ever let myself get that way? Not on your life. I'm going to rise above it. I'm going to become so great and famous, I won't *have* to fall in love.

ALAN   (*With a smile, begins to leave*)   Good luck, Millie.
(FLO *comes to the door, a bereaved expression on her face*)

FLO   Oh, Alan! (ALAN *stops*) Won't you come to dinner tonight? I'm having sweet-potato pie and all the things you like, and . . .

ALAN   Dad has been wanting to go on a fishing trip, Mrs. Owens. I guess we'll be gone.

FLO   Gone?

ALAN   Yes, I may be gone for quite a while, Mrs. Owens.

FLO (*Sensing the end has come*)   Oh, Alan!

ALAN   Tell Madge I hope she'll be very happy.

FLO   Alan, you're coming back, aren't you?

ALAN   To tell the truth, Mrs. Owens, Dad has been arranging a job for me in Chicago . . .

FLO   Chicago!

ALAN   . . . so I may not be back home for quite a while.

FLO   Oh, Alan! Madge is going to be broken-hearted.

ALAN   I don't think so, Mrs. Owens. Not really.

FLO   Oh, she *will,* Alan. You just don't know how she . . .

ALAN   Madge will never feel broken-hearted about *me.*

FLO   Oh, Alan, I think I'm going to cry.

ALAN   Goodbye, Mrs. Owens. Goodbye, Millie.
(*He hurries off.* FLO *and* MILLIE *watch him drive away. The sound of the powerful engine of his car fades in the distance*)

FLO   He's gone.
(*Now* MRS. POTTS *comes walking back with her dollar bill*)

MRS. POTTS   (*Breathless*)   I couldn't catch him. He'll think I was just a stingy old woman.

FLO   (*Her anger returned*)   A young lout like him, who never had a dollar to his name, never will have, is not gonna miss one, one way or the other.

MRS. POTTS   I hate to keep something that was right- fully his. Here, Millie, you take the dollar and have a good time.

MILLIE   Gee, thanks!
(*Now the wedding party comes out,* HOWARD *and* ROSEMARY, IRMA *and* CHRISTINE *dancing around them like flower girls, tossing rice out of a paper sack.* MRS. POTTS *takes a moment or two to catch on, then joins the festivity, throwing her share of rice, too. As the party progresses forward,* MADGE *can be seen looking wistfully out the front door,* MILLIE *looks on a little wryly*)

ALL   You're getting a wonderful girl, Howard Bevans!
       May all your troubles be little ones!
       Be happy forever and ever!

IRMA   Girl, are you wearing something old?

ROSEMARY   Yes, I'm wearing an old pair of nylons, but
    they're good as new.

IRMA   Here's my handkerchief, girl. You can borrow it.

ROSEMARY   I'll give it back to you, Irma. Thanks.

CHRISTINE   She hasn't got on anything blue, Irma.

IRMA   Oh, kid!

ROSEMARY   Yes, I have.

IRMA   I don't see it.

ROSEMARY   And you're not gonna!
    (*This is considered very daring and they all laugh*)

FLO (*To herself*)   Who am I gonna rent her room to?

ROSEMARY   Mrs. Owens, I left my hot-water bottle in
    the closet and my curlers are in the bathroom. You
    and the girls can have 'em. I surely want you to
    know I've appreciated such a nice place to stay. It's
    been just like home, and in some ways . . . you've
    been like a mother.
    (*She begins to blubber a little*)

FLO (*Civilly*)   Thank you, Rosemary.

ROSEMARY   I stored the rest of my things in the attic.
    I'll come after them when we get back from our
    honeymoon. Cherryvale is not far away. We can be
    good friends, same as before. Goodbye, Millie!
    (*She kisses* MILLIE *on cheek*)

MILLIE   G'bye, Miss Sydney!

ROSEMARY   And goodbye, Madge! (*Turns to* MADGE, *who is standing in the doorway, and kisses her on cheek*) Isn't Madge pretty, girls?

IRMA *and* CHRISTINE   Oh, yes!

ROSEMARY   I always said Madge Owens is the prettiest girl in town.

FLO   Know anyone I can rent your room to?

ROSEMARY   Linda Sue Breckenridge! She's the sewing teacher. She and Mrs. Bendix had a fight. Mrs. Bendix wanted to charge her twenty cents for her orange juice in the morning and none of us girls ever paid more'n fifteen. Did we, girls?

IRMA *and* CHRISTINE   No. Never.

ROSEMARY   Irma, you tell Linda Sue to call Mrs. Owens.

IRMA   I'll do that very thing.

ROSEMARY   You've been a wonderful friend, Mrs. Potts.

MRS. POTTS   Happy days, Rosemary!

ROSEMARY (*Now a complete flood of tears*)   Goodbye, Irma and Christine! I'm gonna miss you girls. We had some awfully jolly times together.

IRMA   I hope you're happy, girl. I mean it.

HOWARD (*A little restless*)   All set?

ROSEMARY (*All her tears vanish as* HOWARD *takes her arm, and the wide smile is back*)   All set and rarin' to go!
(*All are merry now*)

ALL   Happy wedding day!
       You're a handsome pair!
       May all your troubles be
       little ones!
       Be happy!
       You're getting a wonder-
       ful girl, Howard Bevans!

HOWARD   (*Privately to* FLO) A man's gotta settle down sometime.

FLO   Of course!

HOWARD   And folks'd rather do business with a married man.

ROSEMARY   (*Takes* HOWARD'S *arm, starting down the walk.* MRS. POTTS, IRMA *and* CHRISTINE *follow, throwing rice.* MILLIE *and* FLO *remain on the doorstep.* MADGE *lingers in doorway*) Where we goin', Howard?

HOWARD   I gotta stop in Cherryvale first and pack a bag.

ROSEMARY   Aren't we goin' on a honeymoon?

HOWARD   Thought we'd take a little trip through the Ozarks.

ROSEMARY   Oh, I love the Ozarks!

ALL   How nice!
       The Ozarks are lovely this time of year.
       May all your troubles be little ones!
       Two's company on a honeymoon.

HOWARD   I got a cousin over there. He and his wife run a tourist camp. They'll put us up, maybe for free.

ROSEMARY   (*Relishing every word*) Lord, I feel like an old married woman already.

ALL   (*As* ROSEMARY *and* HOWARD *walk off to his car*) I never saw a prettier bride.
       Howard Bevans, you're a lucky man.
       May all your troubles be little ones!
       (*They are gone now and everyone's spirits suddenly*

sink as they wave their final goodbyes; and HOWARD'S *car is heard pulling away*)

IRMA   We'll be late for school, Christine.

CHRISTINE   Goodbye!
  (*She waves to the others and hurries off with* IRMA)

FLO (*On the doorstep as* MRS. POTTS *makes her way back to the porch*)   If you ask me, it's a good thing *that* girl got married.

MRS. POTTS   I feel sorry for Rosemary.

FLO   You feel sorry for everyone.

MRS. POTTS   I hope they'll be happy.

FLO   Just the idea of being married'll keep her happy for a long time to come. (*After a moment*) I'm disgusted with you, Helen Potts.

MRS. POTTS   Why?

FLO   You liked that young man, didn't you?

MRS. POTTS   Yes, I did.

FLO   Really!

MRS. POTTS   It was a joy having him in the house.

FLO   Hmmm.

MRS. POTTS   With just Mama and me in the house, I'd got so used to things as they were, everything in its right place, occasionally a hairpin on the floor and the smell of face powder and Mama's medicines, the sachet in the drawers and the geranium in the window . . .

FLO   And I'll keep things the way they are, in *my* house.

MRS. POTTS Not when a man is there, Flo. He sat at the table and suddenly everything was different. There was a clean smell of laundry soap and coarse linen, and some sort of nice hair oil and shaving lotion . . . and there he was talking in a full voice that I feared would shake the ceiling, 'cause Mama and I always whisper; and he took the dainty napkin I gave him and wiped the jam off his mouth without dabbing, the way Mama and I do. Then when he walked up the stairs in his boots, he made a clatter and you *heard* him. Everything he did made you know there was a man in the house, and it seemed good.

FLO That's a matter of opinion.

MRS. POTTS And knowing there's a man in the house reminded me . . . I'm a woman. And that seemed good, too.

FLO Did it?

MRS. POTTS Yes. Only some women . . . don't like to be reminded.

FLO (*After considering the remark for a moment*) Well, we've said goodbye to Alan Seymour.

MRS. POTTS I'm awfully sorry, Flo.

FLO If you expect happy endings anywhere outside the movies, you're fooled.

MRS. POTTS There are other nice boys in town, Flo.

FLO Name one.

MRS. POTTS I'm sure there are.
(*Now from inside comes the sound of a furious* MILLIE, *who is heaping her insults on* MADGE, *calling her* slut *and* floozy)

FLO   Girls, stop it this instant. We've given the neighbors enough to talk about for one day.
(*Now* MILLIE *comes strutting out with her school
books*)

MILLIE   My own sister, an old floozy. That's all she is,
an old floozy.

FLO   Watch your language.

MILLIE   She's nuts about that crazy guy. She's mooning
around the house like a sick cat.

FLO   Mind your business and go to school.

MILLIE   I don't see why I can't have Miss Sydney's
room, now she's gone.

FLO   'Cause we need the rent money, that's why.

MILLIE   I'd certainly like to have one spot in this house
I could call my own.

FLO   Are you going to school looking like that?

MILLIE   Why shouldn't I go to school looking like this,
pray tell?

MRS. POTTS   But you were pretty last night, Millie.
Pretty as a picture.

MILLIE   Maybe I didn't feel so pretty.

MRS. POTTS   You'd be pretty now if you put on a dress
and rubbed a little color in your cheeks.

MILLIE   And have Venus de Milo in there think I was
giving her competition?

FLO   Well, it's your life.

MILLIE   You're damn right. And I say phooey on all
this "pretty" business. I'm gonna be a great writer and
a writer doesn't have to be pretty.

FLO   A great writer could at least put on a clean shirt. It's the first day of school. You should look respectable.

MILLIE   I don't care what anyone thinks in this town. When I graduate from college, I'm going to New York; and I'm gonna write novels that'll shock people right out of their senses.

FLO   What could *you* write a novel about?

MILLIE   *You'll* find out.
(*Off stage, a boy's voice provokes* MILLIE)

VOICE   Hey Goon-Girl!

MILLIE   (*Spotting him in the distance*)   It's Poopdeck McCullough. He thinks he's so smart.

FLO   Keep peace and let him think so.

VOICE   Hey Goon-Girl! Come kiss me. I wanta be sick.

MILLIE   That no-good bastard.

FLO   Millie!

MILLIE   If he thinks he can get by with that, he's crazy. (*An evil glint in her eye, she picks up a stick with which to chastise her offender*) I'll get *you!* I'll get even with you if it takes the rest of my life.

FLO (*Trying to stop* MILLIE)   Millie! Millie! (*She gives up and sits down again, and takes up her sewing. Now* MADGE *comes out looking very solemn, ready to start for work. The train whistles in the far distance now, a faint reminder.* MADGE *listens*) You better get to work. There'll be no more Alan to come by for you in a shiny Cadillac.

MADGE   I can walk. It'll be good for my figure.

FLO (*Disparagingly*) Back to your job at the dime-store, selling chocolate drops and honey bars to all the riffraff in town.

MADGE (*Peacefully*) I like my job all right.

FLO You gotta hang onto it now. We're gonna need the money. So don't be late.

MADGE If I smile at Mr. Hendricks, he doesn't mind if I'm late.
(*Inside, the telephone rings*)

FLO You're up. You get it.
(MADGE *goes inside. A police siren is heard racing to a stop*)

MRS. POTTS Oh, dear! It's the police. You don't need the police now, do you, Flo?

FLO No.

MRS. POTTS (*Running out to greet them*) We don't need you now, Mr. Policeman. It was all a mistake. We don't need you. (FLO *sits alone looking rather stony as* MRS. POTTS *makes her way back*) A person could be robbed of house and home before the police in this town ever got to him.

FLO (*With distaste*) Love!

MRS. POTTS But it's natural to fall in love, Flo. I read an article in the *Reader's Digest* by some famous psychiatrist, trying to persuade people it's *natural* to fall in love.

FLO A woman falls in love and where is she?

MRS. POTTS I guess, once she falls in love, the question never bothers her.

MRS. POTTS' MOTHER (*Off stage, calling*) Helen! Helen!

MRS. POTTS (*Jumping up*) Oh dear! (*Calls back*) I'm over at Flo's, Mama. You don't need me.

FLO (*As* MRS. POTTS *returns*) When I think of the life she *could* have had, surrounded by all the beautiful things money can buy.

MRS. POTTS Madge is beautiful herself. She doesn't need those things.
(*Now* MADGE *comes back out*)

FLO (*Quizzically*) Who was it?

MADGE Lou Connors.

FLO Who's he?

MRS. POTTS He's that handsome boy that takes tickets at the movie, Flo. I pointed him out to you when we went to see *Ben-Hur*. Remember? He has rosy cheeks, and he looks so splendid in that blue uniform.

FLO What'd he want?

MADGE A date.

FLO What'd you tell him?

MADGE I told him I'd think about it sometime.

FLO You better get to work.
(MADGE *stands on the doorstep, looking at herself in her compact mirror, not with vanity but just to make sure that no carbuncles have appeared in the last few minutes.* JOKER, *a good-looking lad, a filling station attendant dressed in coveralls and jaunty cap, saunters by. He stops before the house and smiles at* MADGE *challengingly*)

JOKER Hi, Madge!

MADGE (*A little surprised*) Well . . . hi, Joker!

JOKER Goin' to work?

MADGE   I guess . . . not for a while, Joker.

JOKER   I just happened by. I'm on my way to the filling station.

MADGE   Are you?

JOKER   I . . . I thought we might walk together.

MADGE   I guess I'm not ready, Joker. Not yet.

JOKER   (*Lightly*)   O.K! I'll get you sometime when you're ready.
(*He saunters off, his hands in his hip pockets. He is whistling*)

FLO   He just *happened* by. He lives on the other side of town.

MRS. POTTS   All the boys like Madge.
(*Now a gang of* BOYS *in a stripped-down jalopy drive by, honking the horn and hollering at* MADGE. *The radio in their car blares out blatant jazz. They sound like a cheering squad*)

BOYS   Hey, Madge! How ya like the hot rod? Where you goin'? C'mon, get in! Hey, beautiful! Hey, gorgeous! Where you goin'?

FLO (*Looking over her glasses*)   Who *are* those boys?

MADGE   Some of the gang.

FLO   Young loafers! Why aren't they in school or at work?

MRS. POTTS   They're coming back. They're driving up and down the street.

BOYS   Hey, beautiful! Where you goin'? C'mon in! We're waitin'!

FLO   It's a nice day. You walk.

MADGE   I'm perfectly capable of making up my own mind, thank you.

FLO (*Outraged*)   Well, I like that!

MRS. POTTS   Yes, Flo. Let her make up her own mind. You don't have to worry about Madge.

FLO (*Having to give up again*)   I just can't *help* worrying.

MRS. POTTS   Madge is a woman now, Flo. She's not a girl any more.

BOYS   Hey, Madge! Hey, good-lookin'! Where you goin'? C'mon, get in. Where you goin'?

(*The* BOYS *make a sort of choral background for* MADGE, *their radio sending forth hot blasts of brassy jazz, as* MADGE, *with a sort of peaceful equanimity, goes down the walk and starts for work.* FLO *and* MRS. POTTS *watch for a long time*)

FLO   Can you see from here? Did she get in the car?

MRS. POTTS   No. She's still walking.

FLO (*Still disgruntled, picks up her sewing basket*)   I better get to work.

BOYS (*Their voices echo far in the background now*)
                    Hey, beautiful!
                    Where you goin'?
                    We're waitin'.
                    C'mon, get in.
                    Hey, gorgeous!
                    Where you goin'?
                    Where you goin'?
(*The echo of their voices fills the stage*)

Curtain

*

TO BOBOLINK,
FOR HER SPIRIT

* *

Every day the weather permits, a group of autograph hunters assembles outside the 21 Club in New York. The size of the group varies from day to day and seems to depend upon the number and magnitude of the movie stars reported to be inside. It is an oddly assorted group, most of them teen-agers, but sometimes middle-aged women are included. The ringleader of today's group is BOBOLINK BOWEN, *a woman probably in her early thirties, who is so fat that her body, in silhouette, would form an almost perfect circle.* BOBOLINK *has the fat woman's usual disposition, stolidly complacent and happy. Her lips usually are formed in a grin of guzzling contentment. Her hair is short and kinky; she wears thick-lensed glasses that reduce her eyes to the size of buttonholes, and her clothes by necessity are simple: a man's coat-style sweater, saddle shoes and bobbysocks and bare legs that swell at the calves like bowling pins.* NELLIE, *a starved and eager woman in her late twenties, is* BOBO-LINK'S *dependable stand-by. The two young boys,* RENALDO *and* FRITZ, *are friends; the two young girls,* GRETCHEN *and* ANNAMARIE, *are friends also. They are people without any personal attraction they could possibly lay claim to, and so must find in others attributes they want and lack in themselves.* ANNAMARIE, *in her dress, has tried to emulate one of her favorite film stars; she wears exotic sun glasses, a complicated coiffure and exciting shoes with straps, bows and platform soles. The group has been standing around for over an hour. They have learned to handle these periods of waiting like patients in a rest home; they talk idly with one another, move restlessly about in a limited space.* GRETCHEN *knits,* FRITZ *is working a crossword puzzle. Behind them stands the* DOORMAN, *a man of rigid and calculated dignity, dressed in a colorful uniform. He holds his head high and keeps it turned away from the autograph seekers as though to disclaim any association with them.*

RENALDO　I heard Lana Turner was in this joint last week. Man, wouldn't that be something?

FRITZ　Just imagine walking down the street one day and . . . plop! all of a sudden there's Lana Turner . . . just outa the blue. Man, I'd drop my teeth.

NELLIE　(*Making a claim that* BOBOLINK *would be too proud to make for herself*)　Bobolink here's got Lana Turner's autograph. Haven't you, Bobby?

BOBOLINK　Lana's no better'n anyone else.

FRITZ　(*Impressed; to* BOBOLINK)　No foolin'? You got Lana Turner's autograph?

BOBOLINK　(*Proving it with her autograph book*)　Think I was lying to you?

FRITZ　(*To* RENALDO)　Look, Ronny, she's got it.

NELLIE　Oh, Bobolink's got 'em all.

BOBOLINK　(*She always holds her own*)　I got all of 'em that's worth gettin'.

GRETCHEN　My girl friend saw her. My girl friend goe out to California every summer. Her folks are rea wealthy. She saw Lana Turner on the beach one da

and she just goes up to her and says, "Hi, Lana" . . .
just like that. And Lana smiles back and says, "Hi!"

BOBOLINK   Sure, she's not stuck-up. Now Katharine
Hepburn's stuck-up, but Lana Turner's not at all. The
best ones never are stuck-up.

FRITZ (*Addressing the* DOORMAN, *who stands with rigid
dignity*)   Hey, mister, how long's Perry Como been
inside?
(*The* DOORMAN *does not respond*)

BOBOLINK (*To* FRITZ)   Hey, don't you know anything?
Those guys don't pay no attention to movie stars.
They see so many of 'em they get sick of 'em. You
can't find out anything from him.

FRITZ   Are we sure Perry Como's there?

BOBOLINK (*Impatiently*)   I told you I seen him, didn't
I? Well, what more do you want? I was up there on
the corner waitin' for a bus. Nellie here nudges me and
says, "Hey, ain't that Perry Como goin' into the 21
Club?" And I looked and sure enough. There was a
guy goin' in, had on the same kinda suit Perry Como
had on last week over at the Paramount. Looked
exactly like him.

FRITZ   But are you sure it was him?

BOBOLINK   Look, boy, you're never sure of anything in
this world, don't you know that?

FRITZ   We been waiting here over an hour.

BOBOLINK   No one's asking you to stay. I waited outside
the Stork Club three hours one night, three whole
hours, and it was snowin'. Someone told me Elizabeth
Taylor was inside and I wanted her autograph. It
wasn't Elizabeth Taylor at all. Just some college girl

trying to make out she was Elizabeth Taylor. I was sore, but what the heck!

NELLIE   Besides, you never know what's going to happen in this racket; like the time we was waitin' outside the St. Regis for Ronald Colman, and shoot! Who cares about Ronald Colman . . .

RENALDO   He's famous.

NELLIE   Not very. Anyway, we was waitin' for his autograph and . . .

BOBOLINK (*Taking over*)   Oh, yeh, and we'd been waiting for Ronald Colman all night and we was just about to give up and go home and then what do you think happened?
(*She's going to build up suspense by making them guess*)

NELLIE   That was the best luck we ever had, wasn't it, Bobby?

BOBOLINK   Well, we was just about to give up and go home when a taxi draws up at the curb and Van Johnson and Peter Lawford get out, and we got 'em both, right there on the same spot.
(*This is an impressive story. The others are a little awed*)

GRETCHEN   No foolin'! You got Van Johnson and Peter Lawford?

BOBOLINK (*She produces her autograph book proudly*)   And both at the same time!

NELLIE (*Producing her own evidence*)   I got 'em, too.

BOBOLINK   See what Peter Lawford wrote? "All my love to Bobolink." I told him that was my name.

NELLIE   And he said the same thing on mine, but my name's Nellie. They're both just as cute in real life as they are in pictures, aren't they, Bobby?

BOBOLINK   Not a bit stuck-up.
(*An elaborately dressed couple appears in the doorway coming out of the restaurant. The woman wears a dress of dramatic cut and an exotic hat. Their manner is ridiculously aloof and they make quite a thing of ignoring the autograph hounds*)

FRITZ (*Nudging* RENALDO)   Hey, who's that?
(*They all look*)

GRETCHEN   Looks like Rosalind Russell, don't it?

BOBOLINK   Naw, that ain't Rosalind Russell. I seen Rosalind Russell. She's real tall.

ANNAMARIE   Isn't she stunning? Don't you just love that dress?

GRETCHEN   I bet that dress cost two or three hundred dollars.

ANNAMARIE   'Course it did. Probably cost more than that.
(BOBOLINK *is studying the woman, trying to decide who she is. The woman and her escort now stand at the curb waiting for the* DOORMAN *to hail them a cab. The hounds are gaping at them*)

FRITZ (*Approaching the glamorous woman*)   Miss, can I have your autograph?
(*The woman is a little surprised. She looks questioningly at her escort, who gives her an indulgent smile. So the woman, a little mystified, signs her name to* FRITZ'S *book. Then she and her escort disappear in a cab.* FRITZ *studies the signature. The others flock around him to see who it is, but* BOBOLINK *is not as quickly curious as the others*)

ALL   Who is she? Hey, let's see. It's not Rosalind Russell, is it? If I missed Rosalind Russell, I could kill myself. Let's see.

FRITZ   I'm trying to make it out. (*He attempts a pronunciation of the name*) Irina Nechibidikoff.

BOBOLINK   (*Emphatically*)   Russian!

FRITZ   Hey, she may be someone famous.

BOBOLINK   Whoever heard of Irina Nechibidikoff?

ANNAMARIE   Maybe she's a famous dancer.

BOBOLINK   So what? She's not in the movies, is she? With a name like that.

GRETCHEN   Maybe she's a famous singer.

FRITZ   Anyway, I got her, whoever she is.

BOBOLINK   I'm waitin' here for Perry Como. I come for Perry Como, and I'm gonna stay till I *get* Perry Como.

NELLIE   (*To the others*)   Bobby always finishes up what she starts out to do.

BOBOLINK   You tell the world I do. And I'm not leavin' here without Perry Como's autograph. I been trailin' him for two years. I got Bing Crosby; I got Frank Sinatra; I got Van Johnson and Peter Lawford and Jimmy Stewart and Tyrone Power . . .

NELLIE   Tell 'em about the time you got Tyrone Power, Bobby.

BOBOLINK   Now I mean to get Perry Como. He's not my favorite or anything, but I want to get his autograph.

NELLIE   Tyrone Power's your real favorite, isn't he, Bobolink?

BOBOLINK (*With modest adoration*)   Yah. Tyrone's a real guy.

NELLIE (*To the others*)   Bobbie's president of the Tyrone Power Fan Club up in Irvington. (*The others are impressed*) Go on, Bobbie, tell 'em about Tyrone.

BOBOLINK (*This is too sacred to be treated lightly and* BOBOLINK *is capable of dramatizing her modesty*) No, Nellie, I don't think it's right a person should go around boasting about things like that.

NELLIE   Tell 'em, Bobby. If you don', I will. (BOBOLINK, *after all, can't stop her*) Bobby's too modest about it, I think. But Tyrone Power shook her hand and told her personally that he was very indebted to her . . .

BOBOLINK   I met him at the train; don't forget that, Nellie.

NELLIE   As president of the Tyrone Power Fan Club in Irvington, she met his train at the Pennsylvania Station when he came in from Hollywood.

BOBOLINK   And I had to fight the man at the gate to let me pass.

NELLIE   That's right. She did. See, it wasn't supposed to be known that Tyrone was on that train, but the Pasadena Fan Club had wired us he was coming, so Bobby and I met him at the train to welcome him to New York, didn't we, Bobby?

BOBOLINK   We didn't want him t'arrive in town all alone.

NELLIE   'Course not. So we went down to the station together. The man at the gate wouldn't let us through, but Bobby got by him, didn't you, Bobby? I had to stay behind, but Bobby got through and got right on the train, didn't you, Bobby?

BOBOLINK   And I hunted all through them cars till I found him. He was still packing his things and he was in a hurry.

NELLIE   But he wasn't stuck-up, was he, Bobby?

BOBOLINK   (*This is sacred to her*)   No, he wasn't stuck-up at all. I introduced myself as the president of the Irvington Fan Club, and told him we had forty-three members and met once a week to discuss his career.

NELLIE   And he was very pleased, wasn't he, Bobby?

BOBOLINK   Of course he was. And I told him us fans was awful glad he didn't marry Lana Turner 'cause, although our club don't have anything personal against Lana Turner, we never did think she was the right sort for Tyrone. And I told him that in just those words.

NELLIE   And she isn't. I mean, I like Lana Turner and I think she's awfully pretty and of course she's awful famous, but she isn't the right sort of girl for Tyrone at all.

GRETCHEN   And you got his autograph?

BOBOLINK   'Course I got his autograph, silly. Nellie did, too. And he gave me lots of his autographs to give to other club members, but he made me promise not to give them to anyone else. (*She displays her proudest acquisition*) Just club members. Then he told me to call him Tyrone, and he said he was very indebted to me. See what he wrote?

FRITZ   (*Reading the inscription aloud*)   "To Bobolink, for her faithful enthusiasm and spirit." Gee!

BOBOLINK   Then he had his secretary give me a picture and he autographed it, too. It just says, "With gratitude, Tyrone." Then he shook my hand and he said he wished he could come to Irvington to visit the fan club, but he was going to be terribly busy in New York, he wouldn't have a minute to spare, and then he had to get back to Hollywood to make another picture.

ANNAMARIE *(To* NELLIE)   Did you meet him?

NELLIE   No, but I saw him. He came hurrying through the gate with his coat collar turned up so no one would recognize him. I called out, "Hi, Tyrone! I'm a friend of Bobolink," but he started running.

BOBOLINK   He didn't want people to know who he was. Sometimes they get mobbed by fans and get their clothes ripped off and even get hurt. I wouldn't want anything like that to happen to Tyrone.
(Another couple appear in entrance way. The young man is dapper and handsome and the girl is pretty and expensively dressed. The haughty DOORMAN *starts hailing a cab)*

RENALDO   Hey, who's this?

GRETCHEN   Is this Perry Como?

BOBOLINK *(With a look)*   No, that ain't Perry Como.

NELLIE   She looks familiar, don't she? I bet she's in pictures.

BOBOLINK *(After a moment's study)*   No, she ain't in pictures.

FRITZ   They might be somebody. They might be somebody we haven't heard about yet. *(The couple stand at the curb now.* FRITZ *approaches them)* Mister, can I have your autograph?

ANNAMARIE (*To the girl*)   Are you in pictures?
(*The girl smiles tolerantly and shakes her head no*)

GRETCHEN   Go on and sign anyway, will you please?

ANNAMARIE   I bet you're both in pictures and just don't
wanta admit it. C'mon and give us your autograph.
(*The young man and the girl smile at each other and
sign the books, while the* DOORMAN *hails a cab. But
this is small-time stuff for* BOBOLINK. *She has the
dignity of her past career to think of. She stays back,
leaning against the grill fence surrounding the club,
with a look of superior calm on her face.* NELLIE *stays
by her side*)

NELLIE   I don't think they're anyone famous, do you,
Bobolink?

BOBOLINK   'Course not. I can tell the famous ones. I can
tell.

NELLIE   Sure you can, Bobby.
(*The couple go off in a cab. The* DOORMAN *returns to
his position by the doorway. The young autograph
seekers start studying the names that have been in-
scribed in their books*)

BOBOLINK   They might be famous *one* day . . . I said
they *might* be . . . But I don't have time to waste on
people that *might* be famous.

NELLIE   'Course not.
(*They stand quietly, removed from the others now*)

FRITZ   (*Reading his new acquisitions*)   Frederick
Bischoff and Mary Milton. Who are they?

ANNAMARIE   Yah, who are they?

GRETCHEN   I bet she models. I think I seen her picture
once in an ad for hair remover. Yah, that was her. I

know it was. It was a picture showed her with one arm stretched over her head so you could see she didn't have no hair under her arm and was smiling real pretty.

ANNAMARIE   He's probably just a model, too. He was kinda cute, though.

BOBOLINK (*Personally to* NELLIE, *in appraisal of her colleagues*)   These are just kids, Nellie.

NELLIE   Yah.

FRITZ   Isn't anyone famous ever coming outa there?

RENALDO (*To* BOBOLINK)   Are you sure you saw Perry Como go inside?

BOBOLINK   I said Perry Como was inside, didn't I? If you don't believe me, you don't have to.

NELLIE   Bobolink knows a lot more about these things than you kids do. She spotted Perry Como two blocks away and Bobolink don't make mistakes.

RENALDO   O.K. O.K. Don't get sore.

NELLIE   You might remember that Bobolink is president of the Tyrone Power Fan Club.

FRITZ   We wasn't doubtin' your word. C'mon, Renaldo. Let's wait.

GRETCHEN   Let's wait a little longer, Annamarie.

ANNAMARIE   I gotta get home for supper, Gretchen.

GRETCHEN   Let's wait.

FRITZ (*To* RENALDO)   Let's wait.
(*They resume their positions of patient attendance*)
Curtain

*

PEOPLE
IN THE WIND

* *

The scene of the play is the corner restaurant of a small country town in Kansas. The restaurant serves also as a ticket agency and rest stop for the bus lines operating in the area. It is the last stop on the Greyhound Line from Kansas City to Wichita.

It is close to midnight and the restaurant is empty of customers. It is a dingy establishment with few modern improvements, illuminated by two naked lights hanging from the ceiling on dangling cords. Picture calendars and pretty-girl posters decorate the soiled walls. The atmosphere, like the candied doughnuts under a glass cover on the counter, is left over from yesterday.

Two young women, in uniforms that have lost their starched freshness, are employed behind the counter. ELMA is a scrawny, big-eyed girl just out of high school. GRACE is a more seasoned character in her thirties. A bus is expected in soon and they are checking, somewhat lackadaisically, to see that everything is ready. A tiny radio keeps them supplied with dreamy dance music while they work, and ELMA likes to hum or sing the tunes she happens to know. Outside there is a strong prairie wind that sounds angry with intent to destroy. It comes and goes, creating a great blast against the windows and seeming to shake the very foundation of the frail building, and then subsiding, leaving a period of uncertain quiet.

131

ELMA   Listen to that wind, Grace.

GRACE   (*Unconcerned*)   Yah!

ELMA   (*Going to the entrance to look out the plate-glass window*)   It's blowing things all over the street. It always makes me feel sorta scared.

GRACE   Come back here and help me. The bus is going to be here in a minute and we gotta have things ready.

ELMA   I bet the bus'll be late tonight, with all that wind.

GRACE   Wind don't mean anything to one of those big steel busses.

ELMA   I'd hate to be riding the bus, a night like this.

GRACE   Why?

ELMA   I'd be afraid the wind'd push the bus right off the road into a ditch somewhere.

GRACE   Not one of them big *steel* busses.

ELMA   The wind's awful strong.
    (*Now the bus draws up before the restaurant, its great engine coming to a slow stop*)

GRACE   (*Checking with the clock on the wall*)   Here it is, right on time. I guess the wind didn't push it into no ditch.

ELMA   Just the same, I'm glad I'm not on it tonight. I'm glad I've got my home to go to and a nice warm bed to sleep in.

GRACE   Fill some water glasses, kid. There's fresh coffee. That's about all anyone'll want. The doughnuts are left over from yesterday, but it'll be O.K. to serve 'em. Remember, we got no cheese. We got ham but no cheese.

ELMA (*Dutifully repeating*) No cheese!

(*Now the door swings open and a young* GIRL *enters as though driven. In her early twenties, she is quite pretty in a delicate, blond way. She wears no hat and her hair is blown wild about her face. Her clothes are mainly fragments of finery from a sojourn in Kansas City; a skimpy jacket trimmed with fur, a most impractical dress of sequins and net, and gilded sandals that expose brightly enameled toenails. She lugs in a worn and beaten suitcase which she drops by the door. There is something tense in her demeanor. It takes all her strength to push the door closed again. Then she rushes breathlessly to the counter and solicits the sympathetic attention of* GRACE *and* ELMA, *strangers to her*)

GIRL There's a man on that bus. He's after me. (ELMA *and* GRACE *look at each other*) He'll be in here in a few minutes. Is there any place I could hide?

GRACE Well . . . there's the restroom, honey, but it's out in back.

GIRL In back?

GRACE This is just a country town, honey.

GIRL Oh!

GRACE (*Sizing up the girl*) There's a little hotel across the way, but they'd have to get outa bed to let you in.

GIRL I don't want to be any trouble.

ELMA (*Intrigued*) Is the man somebody you know?

GIRL I never saw him before in my life. He's a cowhand from a ranch somewhere. He's been to Kansas City, riding in the big rodeo and showing cattle. He's mean and crude and . . .

GRACE (*Flatly*) What are you gonna have?

GIRL Coffee, please. Lotsa cream.

ELMA How did you meet him?

GIRL The bus is half empty but he got on and insisted on sitting beside me. I got up and moved and he followed me. Then he followed me again.

GRACE (*Setting a cup of coffee before her*) Here you are, miss.

GIRL He saw my act in the night club in Kansas City. Men are always after me.

ELMA Do you work in a night club?
(ELMA *is fascinated*)

GIRL (*Displaying a slightly shabby pretentiousness*) I'm a singer. I sang at a very exclusive night club there. Our patrons were some of the wealthiest people in Kansas City. I'm on my way to Hollywood now. One of my admirers is a very important man and he has arranged for me to have a screen test, so I'm on my way to Hollywood.

ELMA (*Very impressed*) Gee!

GRACE (*Not so impressed*) Anything to eat?

GIRL No. Nothin' to eat.

ELMA And this man is really after you?

GRACE Get busy, Elma.
(*But* ELMA *doesn't hear her*)

GIRL Don't let on like I told you. He's mean.
(*Now the door blows open and in walks the usual drunk, present on most every night bus. He addresses them as though they were an audience*)

DRUNK   Just *blew* into town and gonna blow right out
again.
(*He considers this very funny and laughs heartily,
weaving his way to the counter, dropping to a stool*)

ELMA (*To the* GIRL)   Is that him?
(*The* GIRL *shakes her head no*)

DRUNK   May I introduce myself to this charming company? I am a very learned professor . . . English lit-
erature . . . a Ph.D. from Harvard . . . Oh yes!
You wouldn't believe it, would you? I wrote my thesis
under Kittredge. My subject was an analysis of the
love element in Shakespeare's plays. I spent six years
writing it. It was published in England. Oh, I am a
very learned man.

GRACE   What'll it be, mister?

DRUNK   I'd like a double shot of rye, if you please,
and . . .

GRACE   I'm sorry but we do not sell intoxicating bever-
ages.

DRUNK   What a shame!

GRACE   What you need is a cup of hot coffee.

DRUNK   My good lady, I have spent a great deal of
money getting into my present merry condition. It
would be a sacrilege to spend ten cents *now* and start
the slow, painful road to sobriety.

GRACE   I'm sorry but we do not sell intoxicating bever-
ages.

DRUNK   You may favor me with a cold glass of Seven-
Up. Yes, I'll have a rare, old bottle of Seven-Up, if
you please. Your best vintage.
(GRACE *reaches into the cooler for the bottle. Two old*

LADIES, *obviously sister spinsters, dressed in black suits and rather Victorian hats, enter and make their way to a table. When the* DRUNK *gets his Seven-Up, he brings a pint bottle out of his pocket and spikes it*)

OLD LADY 1   Let's not go to the counter, Myrtle.

OLD LADY 2   No, we'll take a table.

OLD LADY 1   I feel a little nauseated.

OLD LADY 2   It's the smell of that exhaust. It's sickening.

OLD LADY 1   Do you suppose they could fix me some bicarbonate of soda?

OLD LADY 2   We'll ask them.
(*The two* LADIES *sit at a table. The* BUS DRIVER *comes in, rubbing his hands together. He heads for the counter, addressing the waitresses in a familiar voice*)

BUS DRIVER   Here he is, Girls, your favorite bus driver.

ELMA   Hi, Bud!
(*She is on her way to serve the old* LADIES)

GRACE   Did you bring this wind with you?

BUS DRIVER   No. It brought me.
(*This, too, passes for humor*)

GRACE   Aren't you the comedian!

BUS DRIVER   The bus is doing forty miles an hour, the wind is doing eighty.

GRACE   What'll it be, good-lookin'?

BUS DRIVER   *That's* my girl. Make it a ham and cheese on rye.

GRACE   Sorry, Bud, we got no cheese tonight.

BUS DRIVER   What happened? Did the mice get it?

GRACE (*Laughing*)   Cut it out!

BUS DRIVER   O.K. Make it a ham on rye.

GRACE   Come to think of it, we got no rye, either.

DRUNK (*Interceding*)   I can vouch for that, sir. I asked for rye myself and was refused.

BUS DRIVER   Make it a ham on *some*thing, if you're sure you got the ham.

GRACE   We got ham.
(*The door swings open again, and the* MAN *comes in. He is a big man, probably nearing thirty. It is hard to say whether he is actually good-looking or whether the rugged outdoor character of his person merely gives him a semblance of good looks. He needs a shave. He wears his ranch clothes; a weathered Stetson, dungarees, cowboy boots, plus leather jacket over a flannel shirt open at the throat—clothes he has worn actively in everyday life. He stands in the doorway now, letting the wind rush in around him, till his eye finds the* GIRL)

BUS DRIVER (*Turning to shout*)   Hey, cowboy! Shut that door. (*Back to* GRACE) Guys like that one got no bringin' up. He was probably raised in a barn.
(*The* GIRL *is immediately aware of her pursuer. She cowers over her coffee.* ELMA *finds the* GIRL'S *eyes for an instant to confirm that this is the* MAN. *The* MAN, *meanwhile shuts the door and moves quietly in. He can bide his time. He doesn't have to give the* GIRL *the satisfaction of knowing he is after her. He pretends to ignore her now. He moves over to the magazine rack and thumbs through one of the many lurid periodicals on display*)

OLD LADY 2   Did you pack the presents for Melinda's
children?

OLD LADY 1   They're in my suitcase.

OLD LADY 2   They'll be a year older now.

OLD LADY 1   The baby'll have his teeth.

OLD LADY 2   I wrote Melinda not to meet us. We can
take a taxi to her house.

OLD LADY 1   Can we afford a taxi, Myrtle?

OLD LADY 2   We'll have to, this time of night.
(*Now the* MAN *leaves the magazines and, still pretending indifference, ambles toward the counter.* GRACE
observes a bewitched ELMA, *watching every move the*
MAN *makes*)

GRACE   Get busy, Elma. (*She takes a sandwich to the*
BUS DRIVER) Here you are, Bud. This all the passengers you got tonight?

BUS DRIVER   There's a few more on the bus. They
wanted to sleep.

GRACE   Any trouble?

BUS DRIVER   If this ornery cowboy don't mind his business, I'm gonna put him off.

GRACE (*Meaning the* GIRL)   If you ask me, she's as bad
as he is. She comes in here, handin' me and Elma a
long sob story. It don't fool me. *I* got her number.

BUS DRIVER   He's just a no-account cowpoke.

GRACE   She's just a no-account somethin' else.

MAN (*Finally finds himself beside the* GIRL)   Hi, baby!

GIRL   I don't believe we've met.

MAN   Oh, don't you remember me? I'm the guy sat beside you on the bus out of Kansas City.

GIRL   I still say we haven't met.

MAN   My name's Bo. What's yours? (*She only looks at him scornfully*) I see you brought your suitcase in.

GIRL   Yes, I did.

MAN   Thought you was goin' on to Wichita.

GIRL   I changed my mind.

MAN   (*There's a deep seriousness about him*)   What'd you wanta do that for?

GIRL   I got my reasons.

MAN   Yah? Care to tell me?

GIRL   I don't wish to get off that bus in Wichita with *you*. I know exactly what'd happen. Is that clear?

MAN   What do you think would happen?

GIRL   You're strong. You'd take hold of my arm like you did on the bus, and you'd grip it tight, and you wouldn't let me go.

MAN   And you wouldn't want me to do that, huh?

GIRL   Obviously you have never associated with girls like I. I'm not accustomed to having men mistreat me. I come from a very fine family.

MAN   Yah?

GIRL   And I am an artist, a singer.

MAN   You was sweet, standin' up there before the orchestra, singing your pretty songs.

GIRL   And I told you before, I am going to Hollywood, California, to have a screen test. They want me in pictures.

MAN   Hollywood?

GIRL   Yes.

MAN   I don't believe it.

GIRL   I'm sure it doesn't matter to me whether you believe it or not.

MAN   (*With deep seriousness*)   I thought . . . for a
while there . . . back on the bus . . . you kinda
liked me.

GIRL   I'm sure I have no idea whatever could have given
you such a mistaken impression.

MAN   Didn't you . . . like me?

GIRL   (*Frightened*)   Go way.

MAN   When we was snuggled up in the back seat . . .
you cuddlin' in my arms like a little bird . . .

GIRL   (*Tormented*)   Stop it!

MAN   . . . you was so soft and sweet . . . you *kissed*
me soft and sweet . . .
(*He slowly takes her by the wrist and draws her to
him*)

GIRL   Don't.

MAN   Don't be scared of me, baby.

GIRL   (*Jumping up from counter, frightened, her voice
high and shrill*)   Leave me alone. I'm a respectable
girl. I don't wanta have anything to do with you. If
you don't leave me alone, I'm going to call a policeman.
(*He has not let go of her wrist. He tightens his hold
on it, twisting until a little grimace of pain comes over
her face and she speaks very meekly*)

GIRL   Don't. You're hurting me.
(*Now the* MAN, *disgusted, drops her arm, thrusts his hands into his rear pockets and ambles over to the magazines, avoiding the eyes of the others in the restaurant*)

DRUNK   (*All other eyes in the restaurant are fast on the* MAN *and the* GIRL *and all appear apprehensive, but the* DRUNK *is too immersed in his own phantasies to pay them any attention. He begins, quite unconsciously, to quote poetry*)   "Shall I compare thee to a summer's day?/ Thou art more lovely and more temperate./ Rough winds do shake the darling buds of May,/ And summer's lease hath all too short a date: . . ."
(*He has read the lines with scholarly precision plus an appreciative delicacy of feeling. The others pay no attention; they still are concerned with what is going on between the* MAN *and the* GIRL. *The* MAN *now stands at the magazine rack, his back to them all*)

BUS DRIVER   (*To* GRACE)   I *told* you. He's a bad one.

GRACE   (*With a wise smile*)   Nothin' wrong with him a few lovin' words wouldn't cure.

OLD LADY 1   Maybe the poor girl needs protection.

OLD LADY 2   If she were the right sort of young girl, she wouldn't have got mixed up with him.

GRACE   (*Who seems, for no apparent reason, to dislike the* GIRL, *says to herself or to the* BUS DRIVER)   "They want me for pictures." My foot!

DRUNK   I know all the Shakespearean sonnets by heart. I learned them when I was a lad. (*Turns to the others generously*)   Would anyone care to hear me recite?
(*No attention is paid him*)

BUS DRIVER (*To* GRACE) He's been recitin' poetry the whole trip.

DRUNK (*Subsides into a melancholy soliloquy*) I'm a failure, a poor failure.

GRACE (*To the* DRUNK) Cheer up, mister. Nothin's ever as bad as it seems.

DRUNK I'm not a college professor. I'm not any more. My students used to joke me about my hangovers. One day my students picked me up off the floor and carried me home. "You are a very learned man," I was told by the powers that be. "But we consider you unfit and unable to continue in your profession."

GRACE All you need is just to lay off the stuff, mister.

DRUNK I've always been a very proud man. After all, a man *should* be proud, don't you agree? I loved her very much but I wasn't going to let her know she hurt me. If she didn't have the wisdom and the upbringing to realize my own innate superiority to other suitors, then who was I to humiliate and degrade myself by telling her how very much I cared?

BUS DRIVER (*To* GRACE) Someone oughta put the old boy out of his misery.

OLD LADY 1 I do wish he'd keep quiet, don't you, Myrtle?

OLD LADY 2 A college professor! That's the kind of man we have teaching the young.

DRUNK All I could do was keep my head *high* and leave the scene of action.

MAN (*Has found his way back to the* GIRL) What'd you have to holler out for?

GIRL You hurt me.

MAN   I shoulda given you a beating.

GIRL   You can't talk to me like that. I won't let you.

MAN   You're a spoiled, silly little skirt.

GIRL   I'm not. I'm *not*.
(*She is close to tears*)

MAN   All you wanta listen to is a lot of sweet talk. But
I got no sweet talk. (*Bringing his face next to hers,
looking her square in the eyes*) People got no sweet
talk when they mean business.

GIRL   (*Awed by him*)   You sound so serious.

MAN   It's gonna be you, baby.

GIRL   You're crazy.

MAN   It's gonna be *you*.

GIRL   Sometime I'll get married—when I get out to
Hollywood—to some very handsome young man in a
morning coat. It'll be a big church wedding with lots
of famous people as our guests, drinking champagne,
giving me presents, taking my picture in a beautiful
white dress . . .

MAN   Who you foolin'?

GIRL   I'm not fooling anybody.

MAN   You're foolin' yourself. That's who you're foolin'.

GIRL   You think you know so much.

MAN   (*Whispering softly in her ear*)   I'll not forget how
cute you looked in that night-club place, singin' your
cute songs . . .

GIRL   (*Embarrassed by the intimacy*)   Don't.

MAN   . . . and I'm not gonna forget . . . back there
on the bus . . . before you got mad . . . how you
kissed me . . . sweet and soft.

GIRL   I don't know what made me do it.

MAN   I ain't ever been kissed like that before.

GIRL   (*Torn between desire and confusion*)   Don't.
Please go away. Lemme alone.

MAN   It's gonna be you, baby. I mean business.

GIRL   Don't. The other people are looking.

MAN   I told myself that, when I heard you singin' your
little songs.

GIRL   I told you, I'm on my way to Hollywood. They
want me for pictures.

MAN   (*As though she had not even spoken*)   I been a
hard-workin' man all my life, since I was knee-high.
I had no time for fun like other boys. It's always been
serious with me, everything I ever done. I worked
hard, I saved my dough, I got me the ranch . . . all
mine.

GIRL   I never was on a ranch.
(*She sounds very futile*)

MAN   Now someone's gotta be there with me.

GIRL   Don't, don't.
(*She is tearful*)

MAN   It's gonna be you.

GIRL   I don't know you. You just came in the bus and
sat beside me and took my hand. I never saw you
before in my life. And you're rough and mean and you
haven't even shaved.

MAN   (*A little smile creeps over his face*)   You don't
know how *sweet* a rough, mean guy can be.

GIRL   (*Weakly*)   No . . . no . . .

MAN   Come on, baby. Finish the trip.
(*He stands looking at the* GIRL, *holding her wrist. She avoids his eyes. Now the* BUS DRIVER *gets up and starts for the door, calling on the way*)

BUS DRIVER   Bus headed west! Wichita, next stop! All passengers aboard!

MAN   (*To the* GIRL) We'll get on another bus in Wichita. We'll be there by morning. The ranch house ain't much to look at, baby, but it will be after you get there.

GIRL   I never heard of anything so crazy.

MAN   I'll be waitin' in that back seat, baby. I'll have it all nice and warm.
(*He starts*)

GIRL   (*Getting up*) Just a minute! (*He turns to see what she wants*) With all this fine love talk, you seem to have overlooked one little thing; namely, the sub-ject of gettin' a ring to put on my finger and hiring a man to tell us we're married.

MAN   (*Rather innocently*) Sure.

GIRL   *Sure,* what?

MAN   We'll get married. What kinda guy you think I am?

GIRL   (*Truthfully*) I don't know, mister. I honest don't know.

MAN   (*Going out*) I'll be waitin'.
(*The* GIRL *continues to sit at the counter just looking before her somewhat dazed*)

OLD LADY 1   (*As she and her sister make their way to the door*) Maybe if we help with the work around the house, we can make things easier for Melinda and not get in the way. You can look after the house, Myrtle, and I'll mind the children.

OLD LADY 2   We're always welcome at Melinda's, Clara. Don't worry.

OLD LADY 1   That soda settled my stomach.
(*She gives a polite little burp*)

OLD LADY 2   I'm glad.
(*They go out*)

BUS DRIVER (*To the* GIRL)   Look, miss, if that no-good cowpoke is givin' you any trouble, all you have to do is tell me and I'll see he's taken care of. That's what the police are for, to keep guys like him in their place.

GIRL (*Snapping*)   If I need any help, thank you, I'll ask for it.

BUS DRIVER   Suit yourself. (*Back to the door, calling out*) All aboard, heading west! All aboard!

DRUNK   I'll spend the rest of my life riding on busses. (*Goes to door*) Hear the wind lashing at the houses? But inside that big warm bus, you don't feel it. You're warm and snug, cuddled up in your seat, and you can coast along through the night, sleeping like a baby. With no destination.
(*He goes out*)

BUS DRIVER   See you day after tomorrow, girls.

ELMA   G'night, Bud.

GRACE   Keep the bus on the road.

BUS DRIVER (*One final call*)   All aboard!
(*He looks at the* GIRL *who doesn't respond, then goes out*)

GRACE (*With a little grin of insinuation, to the* GIRL)   Do you still want me to call the policeman, Honey?

GIRL   You can cut out the corny gags.

GRACE   If you're gonna get back on the bus, you better hurry.

GIRL   (*Standing, rearranging herself proudly*)   Who's in a hurry? Let 'em take their time.

GRACE   Them big busses, they're pretty independent. They don't wait on no one. They tell you when they're goin', then they go. And if you're not *on,* it's your hard luck. They're not gonna come back and get you.
(*Now the engine of the bus rises to a roar outside. The* GIRL *hears it and shows her first sign of honest concern. She yanks her suitcase from the corner, seizes open the door and calls out*)

GIRL   Wait a minute. I'm coming. Just a minute.
(*She runs out, letting the door close behind her. Then the bus is heard going off, its motor fading in the distance. All is now quiet*)

ELMA   Gee, sometimes I think I'd like to write a book about the people you see.

GRACE   Wipe off the counter, girl.

ELMA   Huh?

GRACE   The Topeka bus is due in forty minutes. Snap out of it.

ELMA   O.K.
(*She gets busy*)

GRACE   Remind me. Tomorrow we gotta order cheese.

Curtain

A SOCIAL EVENT

*The scene is the bedroom in the home of a young Holly-
wood couple,* RANDY BROOKS *and* CAROLE MASON, *who
have been married only a short time and whose careers
are still in the promising stage. There is abundant luxury
in the room but a minimum of taste. It is late morning
and both* RANDY *and* CAROLE *are asleep, but* RANDY *soon
comes awake, reaches for a cigarette, lights it, and rubs
his forehead discouragedly. Something profound is trou-
bling him. He gets out of bed, slips a robe on and paces
the floor discouragedly. Finally, he presses the buzzer
on the house phone and speaks to the cook.*

RANDY (*Into house phone*) Muriel? We're getting up
now. Bring up the usual breakfast.
(*He hangs up and goes into the bathroom to wash.
Now* CAROLE *wakes up. She too lights a cigarette and
looks troubled. Then she calls to* RANDY)

CAROLE I hardly slept a wink all night, just thinking
about it.

RANDY (*From bathroom*) There's nothing to do but
face the fact that we're not invited.

CAROLE Oh, there's *got* to be a way. There's *got* to be.

RANDY (*Entering*) But, honey, the services start at
noon. It's now ten-thirty.

151

CAROLE Everyone in the business will be there.

RANDY After all, honey, there's no reason to feel slighted. We're both pretty new in pictures. It's not as though we were old-timers who had worked with Scotty.

CAROLE Sandra and Don never worked with Scotty, either. Neither did Debby and Chris, or Anne and Mark.

RANDY I know, honey. We've been through all this before.

CAROLE And I may never have worked with Scotty, but I did meet him once, and he danced with me at a party. He was very nice to me, too, and said some very complimentary things. I met his wife, too. (*An afterthought*) I didn't much like her.

RANDY Maybe I better call Mike again.
(*He picks up the telephone and dials*)

CAROLE What good can an agent do? We're not looking for jobs.

RANDY He may have found some way of getting us invited.

CAROLE I bet.

RANDY (*Into the telephone*) Mike Foster, please. Randy Brooks calling.

CAROLE All the invitations are coming from Scotty's wife. Tell Mike you think there's been an oversight. Maybe he could call her and remind her that you've been referred to in all the columns as "the young Scotty Woodrow," and that Scotty's always been your idol and . . .

RANDY (*Into the telephone*)   Mike? Randy. Look, Mike,
Carole and I still haven't been invited, and I can't help
wondering if there's been an oversight of some kind.
After all, Carole was a great friend of Scotty's and she
feels pretty hurt that she's been overlooked . . . I
never knew him but everyone knows how much I've
always admired him. In an interview just last week,
I said "Scotty Woodrow is still the greatest." Now, I
didn't *have* to say that . . . If you ask me, it showed
a lot of humility on my part to say a thing like that
when, after all, I've got a career of my own to consider . . . Well look, try to do *some*thing, Mike.
Carole and I both should be seen there . . . O.K.,
Mike, call us as soon as you find out.
(*He hangs up*)

CAROLE   He couldn't get us an invitation to Disneyland.

RANDY   He said just Scotty's closest friends are being
invited.

CAROLE   Oh yes! Half the people going, I bet, have
never met him.

RANDY   Well! What are we going to do?

CAROLE   Sandra had an entire new outfit made. Perfectly stunning. And she had the dress made so that
she can have the sleeves taken out later and wear it to
cocktails and supper parties. After all, black is a very
smart color now.

RANDY   Did you tell Sandra and Don we weren't invited?

CAROLE   Of course not. I lied and said we were going.
Now, if we don't get an invitation, I'll have to lie again
and say we came down with food poisoning, or something.

RANDY   How did Anne and Mark get invited?

CAROLE   Mark played Scotty's son in a picture once.

RANDY   When? I don't remember.

CAROLE   A long time ago, before either of us came on the scene.

RANDY   (*Thinks a moment*)   That means Mark's a little older than he admits.

CAROLE   I don't know. The part was very young, practically an infant.

RANDY   Just the same, I'll bet Mark's thirty.

CAROLE   Damn! what am I going to tell Sandra? She invited us to come to her house afterwards and I accepted.

RANDY   (*A little shocked*)   She's not giving a party!

CAROLE   No. She just invited some friends to come in afterwards to have a few drinks and talk about what a great guy Scotty was, and everything. She said she thought we'd all feel terribly depressed. After all, Scotty Woodrow was practically a landmark, or something. Think of it. He's been a star for forty years.

RANDY   Yes. He was really great. It makes me very humble to think of a guy like Scotty.

CAROLE   They say flowers came from the President, and from Queen Elizabeth, and . . .

RANDY   The guest list is going to be published in every paper in the country.

CAROLE   You know, we *could* crash.

RANDY   No, honey.

CAROLE   Who'd know the difference?

RANDY   How would we feel afterwards, when we had to shake hands with Mrs. Woodrow?

CAROLE   She's probably forgotten whether she invited us or not.

RANDY   Honey, I'm *not* going to crash. That's all. I'm *not*.

CAROLE   Everyone would just take it for granted we'd been invited. I mean, we're both just as prominent as Sandra and Don, or any of the others. If you ask me, it'd be a lot better to crash than not to be seen at . . . Well, you can't call it a social *affair* exactly, but it's a social *event*. Anyway, *every*one will be there. *Every*one.

RANDY   It could be some of the others are lying about their invitations, too. You realize that, don't you?

CAROLE   (*Considers this*)   I wonder . . . Well, anyway, they're all going. I *think* they got invitations.

RANDY   I don't know why the studio couldn't have managed it for us with a little pull. They should realize it's in the best interests of my career to be seen there, and my career means as much to them as it does to me.

CAROLE   Same here. Oh, I just don't know how I can face Sandra and Anne and all the others, and make them believe that we really did have food poisoning.

RANDY   You know, we could give ourselves food poisoning. Just a light case. A little rotten meat would do it. Then we'd call the doctor and . . .

CAROLE   (*Horrified*)   No! I'm not going to make myself sick.

RANDY   Just a slight case so you could tell them with a straight face . . . (*A soft tap comes at the door*) Come in. (MURIEL, *the maid, enters with a tray*) Hi, Muriel!

MURIEL   Good morning!

CAROLE   Hi, Muriel. Put it here on the coffee table.
(MURIEL *does as she is told*)

MURIEL   Miss Carole, I hope you remember I told you I'd be gone this morning.

CAROLE   Oh, yes, I'd forgotten. What time will you be back, Muriel?

MURIEL   Oh, I'll be back in time to fix dinner.

RANDY   Is this your day off, Muriel?

MURIEL   No, Mr. Randy. I'm going to Mr. Woodrow's funeral.
(*There is a slight air of superiority about her now.* RANDY *and* CAROLE *look at her with sudden surprise*)

RANDY   Oh . . . is that right?

MURIEL   And after the funeral, Mrs. Woodrow has asked me to join the family at their home.

CAROLE   Muriel, you didn't tell me!

RANDY   Uh . . . were you a friend of Scotty's, Muriel?

MURIEL   My mother worked for him when he was starting out in the business. I was born in Mr. Woodrow's beach house, before he bought that big house up in the canyon.
(*She has thus established herself as near-royalty to* RANDY *and* CAROLE)

RANDY (*Amazed*)   Really?

MURIEL   Oh, yes. Mr. Woodrow was very good to me
when I was a child. Mama worked for him until she
died. I could have stayed on, but after Mr. Woodrow
got married the last time, *she* hired a lot of French
servants I didn't get on with, at all. But they went right
on sending me Christmas cards every year.

RANDY   Uh . . . Muriel, do you have a ride to the
funeral?

MURIEL   No, Mr. Brooks. Mrs. Woodrow's secretary
said I could bring my family, but now that Vincent
has left me and taken the car, I guess I'll have to take
a taxi.

RANDY   Gee . . . that's too bad.

CAROLE   (*Thinking*)   Yes. Isn't it?

MURIEL   (*Starts for the door*)   Well, I have to be getting
ready now. I got a new black dress to wear. All the big
names in Hollywood will be there. I want to look my
best.

RANDY   (*Holding her*)   Uh . . . Muriel, you don't want
to go to the services all alone!

MURIEL   Oh, I don't mind.

CAROLE   Look, Muriel, why don't we all go together?
I mean . . . Well, of course, Randy and I are invited, too, but we'd be glad to go along with you . . .
as your family, you know. Well, after all, you're one
of us, Muriel.

MURIEL   (*Appears to examine the idea*)   All of us go
together, huh?

CAROLE   Of course.

RANDY   I'll drive us all there in the Cadillac.

MURIEL (*This idea appeals to her*)   Oh . . . that'd be
nice.

CAROLE   And then after the funeral, we'll take you to
the house.

MURIEL (*Without sarcasm*)   I see.

RANDY   And you won't have to worry about coming
back to fix dinner.

CAROLE   Of course not.

MURIEL   Well, it suits me. I didn't want to have to call
a taxi. If you folks wanna come along, fine and dandy.
You'll have to pardon me now. I have to get into my
new black dress.

RANDY   We'll meet you downstairs in fifteen minutes,
Muriel.
(MURIEL *exits.* CAROLE *and* RANDY *both jump into
action, getting their clothes out of their respective
closets*)

CAROLE   I told you we'd find a way.

RANDY   Yah. (*Taking a suit from closet*) Say, this suit
could stand a pressing. Do I have to wear black?

CAROLE   Of course, honey. After all, it's a very solemn
occasion.

RANDY   Well, O.K.

CAROLE   I'll have to call Sandra.
(*She picks up the telephone and dials*)

RANDY   It's going to look all right, isn't it? I mean, our
going with Muriel. After all, she's our cook.

CAROLE   Of course. You don't worry about things like
that at a funeral. (*Into the telephone*) Sandra? Carole.
Darling, I'm awfully sorry but Randy and I won't be

able to come to your house after the funeral . . .
Well, you see, we have a duty to Muriel, our cook.
She's the daughter of Scotty's old housekeeper . . .
Yes, Scotty practically raised her. And we feel that
we should take her with us, and then, of course, we'll
have to go to the home afterwards. Just family and a
few of his very closest friends. We can't get out of
it . . . You'll forgive us, won't you, darling? . . .
Oh, it's all going to be terribly sad.

RANDY (*To himself, while dressing*) I guess it'll look
all right. After all, funerals are very democratic affairs.

Curtain

*
THE BOY
IN THE BASEMENT
* *

The setting is an old Victorian house of fussy dignity, kept in the most excellent tidiness and repair. It is in a small mining town close to Pittsburgh. Outside the house, pinned into the ground, is a small, neatly painted sign, "Rest in peace with Scranton. Mortuary." SPENCER SCRANTON, a man nearing fifty, lives in this house with his father and mother, using the house as a funeral parlor as well as a home. Most of the action of the play takes place in the kitchen of the house—a big, clean, white room, with a table in the center. One gets the feeling that the family lives a great deal of its life here, using it as a kind of sitting room, too. At the right end of the room is a stairway leading to the second floor. At the back of the room, a doorway leading to the outside and the garage. At the left of the room, a big bay window and a door leading to the steps into the basement. A small, dark room at the left indicates the basement. It is in darkness until the action moves there. It is then dimly lighted. When the play opens, MR. SCRANTON, SPENCER'S invalid father, is alone onstage, sitting in a big overstuffed chair in the bay window, looking out of the window through his thick-lensed glasses that blur our vision of his eyes and give him an almost inanimate appearance. He is an ancient man, close to eighty, whose life for several years now has been confined to this chair, where he sits like a discarded bride-groom, his only activity looking out of the bay window onto the little bit of world before him. After a few moments, SPENCER comes up from the basement, where he

163

has been at work. There is a troubled look on his face that one feels is there most of the time; it is the expression of a man trying to solve some problem that lies too deeply in his subconscious for him ever to see very clearly. He is a big man with long, hairy arms and big hands, yet with a kind of reluctance about him, as though his very size is an embarrassment to him. His sleeves are rolled up above his wrist, and he looks weary. He goes to the stove, finds a pot of coffee there and pours himself a cup. Then he brings his cup to his father, showing it to him. This is his way of asking his father if he wants some. His father shakes his head slowly, and SPENCER *takes his coffee to the table at center and sits wearily, lighting a cigarette. Now* MRS. SCRANTON *comes down the stairway from above. She is a regal-looking woman in her early seventies, still very alert and active. This is a lovely spring afternoon, and she is dressed to go out. She looks very dignified with her white hair in a neat bun at the back of her head and wearing a simple navy-blue print dress and a small, queenly hat. She is putting on her white gloves as she comes into the kitchen and speaks to* SPENCER.

MRS. SCRANTON   Have you finished with poor old Mrs. Herndon?

SPENCER   Yes.

MRS. SCRANTON   Were the burns real bad?

SPENCER   One whole side of her, raw and purple.

MRS. SCRANTON (*Makes an ugly face*)   Poor old lady. Did you fix her up to look all right?

SPENCER   Yah. Covered her face with grease paint. She looks like a chorus girl now.

MRS. SCRANTON   Son! You mustn't talk disrespectful of the dead.

SPENCER Well, they all get to lookin' pretty much alike. One dead body after another. That's all life gets to be.

MRS. SCRANTON The good Lord doesn't like us to complain. Well, I'm sure you've done a nice job on her. You always do. You're a regular artist in your work. Imagine—burned to death, a poor old critter like her, when her henhouse caught fire. We all have to go sometime, but I pray to the good Lord I won't have to go that way. Her family wants the most expensive funeral, you know.

SPENCER Well, they'll get it.

MRS. SCRANTON Is the organ tuned?

SPENCER Yes.

MRS. SCRANTON Elsie Featheringill is going to sing. I've got to find out what her numbers are. I hope she picks something I won't have to practice. Can the family pay?

SPENCER I guess so.

MRS. SCRANTON I hope so. You're going to need the money, aren't you?

SPENCER What do ya mean by that, exactly?

MRS. SCRANTON After last weekend in Pittsburgh. Turned out to be pretty expensive, didn't it?

SPENCER I told you, I . . .

MRS. SCRANTON Calling me here in the middle of the night, telling me you have to have two hundred dollars wired to you that very minute. What in God's name were you doing that you had to have two hundred dollars that very minute?

SPENCER   I told you, I . . . I had a little trouble with the car . . .

MRS. SCRANTON   You said it was something wrong with the power brakes, but they act just the same now as they did before. Besides, why did the man have to have the money that very minute? Any dependable garage would wait till morning, surely. And besides, you sounded like you'd been drinking.

SPENCER   I . . . I'd had a beer. That's all. Just one glass of beer.

MRS. SCRANTON   I still don't see what you were doing, out until three o'clock in the morning. I certainly wonder at times what goes on those weekends you spend in the city.

SPENCER   What goes on when I leave this house is *my* business.

MRS. SCRANTON   Were you with a woman?

SPENCER   No!

MRS. SCRANTON   No, you never took to women the way your brother did. Well, maybe he taught you a lesson. You see where he's ended up, don't you? A mental hospital for the rest of his life. And what sent him there? Whiskey and women. Whiskey and women.

SPENCER (*As though it were too painful for him to think about*)   Stop it, Mom.

MRS. SCRANTON (*With a nod at* MR. SCRANTON)   It's a wonder he didn't end up the same way, but a stroke got him instead. Something was bound to get him some day.

SPENCER   A-men!

MRS. SCRANTON Well, I've done everything I can for the men in my family. Everything I can. If they choose to go on in their own godless ways, I can't help it. I don't know why you have to keep running into the city every weekend, but I'm not going to plague you about it any more.

SPENCER I just gotta have a change once in a while.

MRS. SCRANTON Lotta good the change does you. You've been jumpy and nervous ever since you got back from that last trip. Something happened there, I guess I'll never know about. Maybe the good Lord is keeping it from me, just to spare me. God knows, I've had enough to put up with in my life. Well . . . (*With a long resentful look at* MR. SCRANTON) I guess my boys didn't come by their ways from any stranger.

SPENCER Don't pick on the Old Man any more, Mom.

MRS. SCRANTON Who says I "pick" on him?

SPENCER You *do*.

MRS. SCRANTON If I hadn't picked on him once in a while, where'd we be now, I'd like to know? Did he have any ambition? No. It was me that made him go to work and earn enough money to send you to school. If it hadn't been for me, we'd be living now in a pigsty. That's the truth. You've got to admit it. (SPENCER *lowers his head in recognition of the probable truth*) Well, I'm going to my meeting now.

SPENCER Have a good time.

MRS. SCRANTON We ladies don't have these meetings to have a good time. We meet to accomplish things. To try to keep some semblance of order in this godless little mining town.

SPENCER What's the meeting about this afternoon?

MRS. SCRANTON Some of us ladies disapprove of some of the movies they've been showing down at the theater. Movies that are too insinuating for our young people to see today. We're going to see to it that these movies are not to be shown any more. We've got the churches behind us, and we're getting the businessmen behind us, too. It's no wonder our young people are making so much trouble today, if that's the kind of thing they see.

SPENCER When'll you be back?

MRS. SCRANTON In time to get your dinner. Good-bye, Son.

SPENCER Good-bye, Mom.

MRS. SCRANTON I'm going to take the Buick.

SPENCER O.K.
(She goes to her husband's chair to speak to him)

MRS. SCRANTON *(In a loud voice, for he is hard of hearing)* I'm going now.

MR. SCRANTON *(He cannot speak, but only makes guttural sounds)* Uh?

MRS. SCRANTON I said I'm going to my meeting now.

MR. SCRANTON Uh?

MRS. SCRANTON Well, never mind.
(She goes out the back door. SPENCER continues sitting by the table, finishes his coffee, then gets up and stretches. MR. SCRANTON makes a series of guttural sounds which draw SPENCER to his side. Apparently SPENCER understands him)

SPENCER   I'm sorry, Pop. There isn't any beer. Her
Royal Highness won't let us keep it. (MR. SCRANTON
makes a sound of annoyance) I'm sorry, Pop. If I
bring home beer, she takes it right out of the ice box
and pours it down the sink. She just won't have it
lying around. (MR. SCRANTON *makes another series of
sounds*) Yah. I'm sorry, too, Pop.
   (*Now* JOKER EVANS *bursts in through the back door.
He is a delivery boy for the supermarket. He carries a
large sack of groceries under his arm and sets it on the
kitchen table. He is a boy of about eighteen, handsome,
husky, full of quick life and humor. There seems to be
a spirit of real camaraderie between him and* SPENCER.
SPENCER'S *face brightens immediately upon* JOKER'S
sudden entrance)

JOKER   (*In a voice that even stirs* MR. SCRANTON)
Supermarket!

SPENCER   Well, hello, Joker, ya li'l bastard!

JOKER   Hi, Spence! Man, it's a great day outside. It's
quit raining now, and it's really spring. Man, it's great
to be alive, a day like this.

SPENCER (*Laconically*)   Yah! Sure!

JOKER   A bunch of us cats are taking dates down to the
river tonight. A wienie roast. Why don't you get a
date, Spence, and join us?

SPENCER (*Chuckles warmly at the foolishness of the invitation*)   Me? Go on a wienie roast with a bunch
of you young punks?
   (*They begin boxing with each other, slapping at each
other good-naturedly*)

JOKER   Sure. Why not? You can be our chaperon. We'd
promise not to do anything you wouldn't do. How's
that?

SPENCER   How do you know what I'd do and what I wouldn't do?

JOKER   Jeepers! You tie one on in Pittsburgh almost every weekend, don't you? Yah, you may act respectable around here during the week, but I'll bet you really throw a ball when you get to the city.

SPENCER   Mind your business, you!

JOKER   Why don't you take me with you sometime, Spence? Huh? How 'bout it? Show me the city, too.

SPENCER   You no-good li'l bastard, I wouldn't take you to a dog fight.

JOKER   Yah? You're scared I'd steal all your women away from you, aren't ya?

SPENCER   Why, you li'l bastard, you couldn't get to first base with the women I see.

JOKER   (*With a total lack of self-consciousness or conceit*) Bet I could. Girls like me. (*Spencer makes a disparaging noise*) No fool, Spence! They *do*. They really like me. Ya know why? They can't boss me. Yah! I'm real independent with 'em. I just take the attitude . . . (*He strikes a pose of boyish boastfulness*) Ho-hum, girls! Here I am. If you like me, I'll see what I can do to make you happy. Now I can't keep 'em off me.

SPENCER   You stuck-up little bastard!

JOKER   I'm *not* stuck-up. I just hold my own, that's all. And man, if you don't learn to hold your own with a girl, she can give you real misery.

SPENCER   You got yourself a girl now?

JOKER   *Do* I? Sue Carmody. Best-lookin' girl in the whole school. Jeepers, I never knew I could fall so hard. We've been goin' together about three months now. She's the greatest. A real good sport, too. Know what I mean?

SPENCER   You going to marry her?

JOKER   I sure wish I could. She wants to get married, but I just gotta get to college if I ever wanta get outa this town. If I married her now, I'd have to stay here and maybe go to work in the mines. I wouldn't like that, and in a few years we'd both be miserable. Sue was trying to hold me at first, but I had a long talk with her and helped her see things my way. She understands how it is now.

SPENCER   She going to wait for you?

JOKER   We talked all that over, too. I don't know if it's fair. By the time I get outa college, I may be in love with someone else. She may be, too. You can't tell about those things. We finally agreed that after I go to college we no longer have any strings on each other, except when I come home for vacations. And while I'm gone, if either of us finds someone we like better, then . . . Well, we'll try to understand.

SPENCER   You talked all this over together?

JOKER   Yah. It was tough to have to face it all. But I decided we'd better be grown-up about things. I didn't wanta go around feeling someone had any strings on me. Know what I mean?

SPENCER   Yah. I know what you mean.

JOKER   And she shouldn't feel I have any strings on her, either.

SPENCER   When did you decide to go to college for sure?

JOKER   Oh, the scholarship came through.

SPENCER   That's swell, Joker.

JOKER (*A little ruefully*)   Yah, but it means I'll have
to play football, and that's kind of a pain. I wanted
to quit that jazz after I got outa high school, and really
settle down and do some work. But if that's the only
way I can get to college, O.K. I'll play football.

SPENCER   What're ya gonna study?

JOKER   Gee, I wanta go into medicine, but I don't know
if I'll be able to make it. I think I can make the grades
O.K. I'm pretty smart, did ya know it? Yah. I'm
graduating this spring in the top five percent of the
class. But I don't know if I'll have the dough. It takes
about three years longer to get through medical school,
and I won't be able to play football then. I'll have to
manage on my own. The folks can't help me much.
I might be able to get another scholarship, though.
Oh well, I won't have to worry about that for a few
years anyway. If I can't make it through medical
school, I'll get myself a job coaching some high school
football team, maybe.

SPENCER (*Deeply serious*)   Gee, kid, I hope you can
make it. It'd be great, you getting to be a doctor.

JOKER   We'd fix us up a system, Spence. I'd kill off all
my patients and send em to *you*.
(*Now they laugh again,* SPENCER *slapping* JOKER *on
the shoulder with rough good nature*)

SPENCER   No thanks. I got more patients now than I
want.

JOKER (*Sobering up*)   I sure don't envy you your job.
I'd think it'd get kinda depressing being around dead
people all the time.

SPENCER (*Melancholy again*) Yah. One dead body after another. That's all my life is.

JOKER How come you never got married, Spence?

SPENCER (*Wishing he could dodge the question*) Oh, I . . . I just never got around to it, Joker.

JOKER You know what? I bet in some ways you never grew up, Spence. No fool! I can have as much fun talkin' with you as with any guy my own age. And I bet you have more fun talkin' with me than you do with all the squares you meet at the Rotary Club . . .

SPENCER That's the God's truth.

JOKER In some ways, Spence, you're like a kid, too. Know it?

SPENCER (*Reflectively*) I suppose.

JOKER (*Looking at the clock on the wall*) Gee, I gotta beat it. I gotta finish my deliveries.
(*He starts for the door as* SPENCER *thinks of something*)

SPENCER Oh, just a minute, kid, before you go off in such a hurry.
(*He digs a wallet out of his pocket*)

JOKER What is it, Spence?

SPENCER I still owe you for washing the hearse for me last Sunday.

JOKER Oh . . . yah. Gee, I'm glad you remembered.

SPENCER (*Handing him a bill*) Here!

JOKER (*Looks at the bill and whistles*) You mean . . . all this, Spence?

SPENCER Sure.

JOKER   Ten bucks? For washing the carcass wagon?

SPENCER   Sure. It was a hard job, all covered with mud.

JOKER   Gee, Spence, you coulda got it done anywhere in town for three or four bucks.

SPENCER   Shut up, ya li'l bastard. If I say it's worth ten bucks, don't bicker with me.

JOKER   (*Deeply touched*)   Sure. Thanks a lot, Spence.

SPENCER   Forget it.

JOKER   I . . . I'll *never* forget it, Spence. Gee, you've always been swell to me.

SPENCER   Get outa here now before I throw you out.

JOKER   Gee, Spence, if there's anything I can ever do for you, anything at all, just let me know, huh?

SPENCER   Sure. Sure. Beat it now.

JOKER   So long, Spence.
   (*He runs out the back door now as* SPENCER *begins putting away the groceries—into the refrigerator, the bread box, and the cupboard. He turns on the kitchen radio, too, and gets a lilting, romantic Viennese waltz that starts him whistling.* MR. SCRANTON *utters a new series of unintelligible sounds*)

SPENCER   What's that, Pop? (MR. SCRANTON *repeats the sounds*) Her Royal Highness is bound to find out. (MR. SCRANTON *makes new noises, somewhat angrily*) Well, I guess it wouldn't hurt either of us to have a short one.
   (SPENCER *opens the basement door and brings out a large bottle of embalming fluid, which he opens; he pours a small snifter full, which he gives to his father. Then he pours one for himself. For a moment, the atmosphere is quite merry. The old man begins nodding*)

his head in rhythm with the waltz, and SPENCER *takes a dustmop from the cupboard, drapes an apron around it and uses it as a dancing partner. He is waltzing about the room when he hears the Buick drive into the garage. Then he returns the mop to the cupboard hurriedly, and puts the bottle of embalming fluid back behind the basement door)*

SPENCER   Her Royal Highness. She's back.

(The old man sobers up and SPENCER *returns to the table, lighting a cigarette and looking very solemn when she comes in. The second we see her, we know she is somehow stricken. It is as though a flash of lightning had parted the skies for a moment and given her a glimpse into some far truth she had never before quite realized, and now she is dumbfounded and horror stricken. She grasps the doorway for support.* SPENCER *looks at her wonderingly)*

SPENCER   Mom, you back already?

MRS. SCRANTON   *(In a hoarse and halting voice)*   I came back as soon as I could . . . after I heard . . . certain things.

SPENCER   *(Frightened by her tone and demeanor)*   Wh . . . what'd you hear, Mom?

MRS. SCRANTON   I heard my dearest friends . . . some of the finest ladies in this town . . . talk about certain things that went on in the city . . . that made my blood chill . . . and made me understand things I never understood before . . .

SPENCER   *(Terrified but trying to conceal it)*   Wh . . . what do you mean, Mom?

MRS. SCRANTON   I was presiding over the meeting, too, and I had to beg them to pardon me. I said I had one of my migraine headaches and had to go home that instant. But I just couldn't sit there and face them any longer. I . . . I don't know how I'll ever keep my head high again, when I walk down the streets of this town.

SPENCER (*Very flustered*) Mom, I . . . d-don't know wh-what you're talking about.

MRS. SCRANTON And to think . . . I raised my son, praying he'd become a great man. I raised both my sons to be great men. No one can say I didn't do my part. And *look* how destiny laughs in my face.

SPENCER Mom, t-tell me.

MRS. SCRANTON (*Spying the book of matches on the kitchen table which Spencer has been using to light cigarettes. She grabs them and forces them in his face*) Where did you get these matches?
(*Her very tone is like a condemnation to hell*)

SPENCER I . . . uh . . . I don't remember, Mom. I g-guess I just picked them up some place.

MRS. SCRANTON The Hi Ho Bar . . . in Pittsburgh. That's where they came from.

SPENCER Yah. I see, Mom. I . . . I don't know *where* I got 'em.

MRS. SCRANTON You got them when you went there last Saturday night, and the place was raided, and you called me for two hundred dollars to pay the policeman to keep him from putting you in jail and to keep your name out of the paper.
(*Her detective work has thoroughly shattered* SPENCER'S *nerves. He can no longer look at her. He cannot even speak. His incoherent grunts give him*

moment's resemblance to his father's mumbling in-articulateness)

MRS. SCRANTON   And the police raided the place because it's a meeting place for degenerates. (SPENCER *collapses over the table, his head in his arms.* MRS. SCRANTON *now has the bearing of a tragic victor*) Dear God, my own son! My own flesh and blood! Corrupting himself in low degeneracy. Going to some disgusting saloon, where men meet other men and join together in . . . in some form of unnatural vice, in some form of . . . of lewd depravity. (*With this,* SPENCER *runs upstairs in panic.* MRS. SCRANTON *now drops to the floor, on her knees, leaning on the table in anguished prayer*) O God, why do you make me suffer so? Why do you thrust every kind of sorrow and humiliation on me to endure? Haven't I always tried to live in your holy light? And haven't I always fought to keep my family there? My loved ones? Why do you continue to punish me, O Lord? I've loved my son since the day he was born and kept him to my breast with loving care. I think I even loved him more than I loved my own husband, for my son's infant love was innocent and pure, and demanded no fleshly act to satisfy its need. O God, will you punish me forever? *I,* who have fought so hard for the *right!* Have fought so hard to keep my mind and heart and body *pure* and free from all physical craving. All my life, I've been a God-fearing woman. Maybe you punish me for sins I don't know anything about. Are you, O Lord? Are you punishing me for sins I know not of? Then tell me, so I can atone for them and be forgiven. I don't want to suffer all my life long. When was the day I did wrong? Dear God, when was the day I did wrong? (SPENCER *comes hurrying down the stairs now, wearing the jacket to his con-servative blue suit, a white shirt, a dark tie and a gray hat. He carries a topcoat over one arm and a suitcase. He has made up his mind what he has to do. He heads straight for the back door,* MRS. SCRANTON *slowly rousing herself to the fact of his leaving)*   Son! Where you going?

SPENCER   I don't know. I'm just goin'.

MRS. SCRANTON   (*Getting up, running to him and grasping his arm*)   Son!

SPENCER   I should have left here a long time ago, but I didn't. I just stayed on, and on, and on. But I'm going now. Never you fear. And it'll be a cold day in hell before I ever come back.

MRS. SCRANTON   Son! Listen to me. Now don't do anything crazy . . .

SPENCER   I suppose it's something crazy if I wanta be my own boss. Forty-six years old. And I stay around here and listen to your yapping. I don't have to do it. See? I'm as free as the next one. I can get a job like that. (*Snaps his fingers*) And live the way I wanta live. And to hell with you!

MRS. SCRANTON   (*Breathlessly*)   I'm your mother, Son. I'm your mother. You can't leave your old home. Now think a minute . . .

SPENCER   (*Loosening her hands on his arm*)   It's no use, Mom. I'm goin'. By God, I'm goin'.
(*He tears out the door*)

MRS. SCRANTON   (*Crying desperately*)   Son! Son! Don't do anything foolish. Come back here, Son. You'll be sorry you left this way. Now come back here and be reasonable. (*But she only hears the sound of the Buick pull out of the garage and drive away. She utters one last futile cry*) Son! (*But he is gone. She drags herself back into the kitchen and drops into the chair by the table*) Oh God, give me peace! Give me peace!

(*She sobs.* MR. SCRANTON *has not moved throughout the scene but has continued staring out the window like a piece of patient wreckage*)

Curtain

scene two

It is early the next morning. The sun is just beginning to show and bring a soft light to the interior of the house. MRS. SCRANTON *is alone onstage, sitting in her husband's chair, looking out of the window but seeing nothing. She is dressed in a long night dress and loose robe, her long, white hair down her back. Her face is stricken with emptiness and grief. She is absolutely immobile for several moments. Then she hears the Buick drive into the driveway, into the garage. A wave of relief comes over her that makes us think for a moment she might faint. But she has never fainted in her life, and she doesn't now. In a few moments* SPENCER *comes in carrying his suitcase, tossing his hat on the post at the bottom of the stairway. He is defeated and knows it. And his bearing tells us he accepts the fact, although sadly. He sets the suitcase down at the bottom of the stairs and stands there, not knowing what to say, hoping his mother will take over the situation. But she doesn't. There is something almost shy about the*

woman now, and her eyes are full and her chin trembles.
Finally, SPENCER *speaks.*

SPENCER   That you, Mom?

MRS. SCRANTON (*Jumps up from her chair and runs to*
   him)   My boy! My boy! My boy!
   (*All the fears and resentments they have fought inside*
   themselves during the past several hours are purged
   now in a fast embrace. Their need, their desperate de-
   pendence on each other, their deep love bring them
   together like lovers)

SPENCER   Mom!
   (*They share a fast embrace. Undoubtedly, this is the*
   only person SPENCER *truly loves*)

MRS. SCRANTON   Oh, my son! Thank God you're back.
   If you hadn't come back, I'd have been ready for the
   basement myself.

SPENCER   Yah. I came back.

MRS. SCRANTON   You won't ever leave me again, will
   you, Son?

SPENCER   No, Mom.

MRS. SCRANTON   Because it's like we'd made a pact together, a long time ago. If one of us breaks it, we're
   both destroyed.

SPENCER   I know it, Mom.

MRS. SCRANTON   I've just been sitting here all night.
   I got your father to bed and then came down here and
   just sat, staring out the window. It's morning now, isn't
   it? Where have you been, Son?

SPENCER   I just drove all over, one town to another. Not
   stopping any place. Just driving. I'm not sure I know
   now where I've been.

MRS. SCRANTON Well, you're back now. That's the important thing. And we're going to try to treat each other nicer now, aren't we? To speak to each other with a little more consideration.

SPENCER Sure, Mom.

MRS. SCRANTON It's just all wrong for us to get so impatient with each other.

SPENCER Sure, Mom.

MRS. SCRANTON (*Sighing deeply*) Oh God, I'm still heaving with relief. (*Upstairs now,* MR. SCRANTON *makes some guttural noises that demand their attention*) Your father's up. You go help him downstairs and I'll get your breakfast. (*Now there is a knocking at the back door*) Oh, it's the body. I took a call for you while you were gone. Some young boy got drowned in the river last night. They said they'd bring the body over first thing this morning. I was too distracted to get the details.

SPENCER One dead body after another. That's all my life is.

MRS. SCRANTON Now, Son, let's not complain.

SPENCER How'd you know I'd be back?

MRS. SCRANTON (*A little hesitantly, with just an edge of guilt*) I . . . I thought . . . you would be. (SPENCER *accepts the minor debasement and her self-confidence, and goes wearily upstairs as* MRS. SCRANTON *opens the back door, admitting two men, dressed as miners, carrying a body on a stretcher, the body covered with a blanket*) Right this way, gentlemen. Over here to the basement door. (*The two silent men carry the body through the kitchen to the basement door, then down the stairs, as* SPENCER *brings his fa-*

*ther down the stairs from the second floor, the old man
hanging onto* SPENCER *with infant dependence, having
to feel his way cautiously every step he takes. Down
in the basement, the two men put the body on a long
white slab, something like a kitchen sideboard, that
drains into a big sink. They keep their heads down in
heavy grief.* MRS. SCRANTON *is talking with them in a
low voice that comes over to the audience as just a
mumble. Their answers to her are monosyllables. She
is a business woman now.* SPENCER *is just getting his
father into the big chair as* MRS. SCRANTON *leads the
two men up from the basement*) Yes, we'll take care
of the dear boy. My son does the best work in town.
You can ask anyone. I know what a grief it is to you,
sudden death always is. But he'll have the boy looking
like he could sit up and speak to you. He'll have a fine
Christian burial. You may depend on that. (*She lets
the two men out the back door now, and turns to
SPENCER*) It's the Evans boy. (SPENCER *gasps*) Deliv-
ered groceries here for the supermarket. The one that
washed your hearse for you sometimes.

SPENCER (*As though to himself*)   No . . . No . . .

MRS. SCRANTON (*Busying herself at the stove, getting
breakfast*)   The little fool, he and a bunch of kids
decided to go swimming last night in the river. Boys
and girls together, going in swimming *naked*. Oh!
That's what they do. Those high school kids have no
shame. What are things coming to? And after all these
spring rains. They might have known what to expect.
Oh, that old devil river gets someone every year.

SPENCER (*Runs down the basement stairs*)   Joker!
Joker! (*He tears the blanket off the young, naked body
and stares at it, unable to believe what has happened.*

Then he returns slowly back up the stairs to the kitchen) Mom! It's Joker! It's Joker!

MRS. SCRANTON   I know. That's what I was trying to tell you. The little fool went in swimming after all these spring rains we've been having. Should have known better. Oh, that old devil river gets someone every year.

SPENCER   (*Can only mutter to himself with a feeling of mysterious loss*)   Joker! Joker!

MRS. SCRANTON   I'm afraid you'll have to get right to work on him. They want the funeral tomorrow. They just want the cheap funeral, too, so don't go to any extra pains. Remember, you've got old Mrs. Herndon's funeral this afternoon at two-thirty. I've got to practice some of Elsie Featheringill's numbers, too. (*Dazed,* SPENCER *returns to the basement and stands beside the body, just staring at it.* MRS. SCRANTON *goes over to her husband's chair and delivers an ultimatum*) There'll be no more whiskey drinking.

MR. SCRANTON   Uh?

MRS. SCRANTON   (*Louder*)   I said there'll be no more whiskey drinking. I found where you were hiding it, in the bottle of embalming fluid.

MR. SCRANTON   Uh?

MRS. SCRANTON   Nothing! How do you want your eggs?

MR. SCRANTON   Uh?

MRS. SCRANTON   I said, how do you want your eggs?

MR. SCRANTON   Uh?

MRS. SCRANTON   (*Giving up*)   Well, I'll poach them. They're easier on the digestion.

MR. SCRANTON   Uh?

MRS. SCRANTON (*Shouting*)   Nothing! (*To herself now, returning to stove*) You don't *want* to hear me. You never did want to hear me. I could holler my lungs out and you still wouldn't hear me.
(*She is busy getting breakfast.* MR. SCRANTON *looks out of his window on a sunny morning, birds twittering now in the trees.* MRS. SCRANTON, *contented as a new bride, sings "Rock of Ages" as she gets breakfast. Down in the basement,* SPENCER *finally moves from his frozen stance at* JOKER'S *side to rub one soft hand warmly over the boy's chest, as though it were precious metal*)

SPENCER (*In a tone of reverence and awe*)   Joker, you little bastard! I never expected to see you down here. Why couldn't you have been more careful, boy? You were alive. Didn't you appreciate it? Most of us are just pretending, and it don't matter when we end up down here. But you were alive. You were alive. Jesus! And I wanted you to stay that way.
(MRS. SCRANTON, *a little curious as to what is going on, sticks her head in the basement door and calls down*)

MRS. SCRANTON (*Suspiciously*)   What are you doing down there?

SPENCER   You'd be suspicious if I was in the same room with a stuffed owl.

MRS. SCRANTON   Don't be sassy. (SPENCER *has no retort*) You can eat your breakfast while he's draining, can't you?

SPENCER (*In a firm voice*)   I won't want any breakfast.

MRS. SCRANTON   Oh, well you'll want coffee. It's ready. Do you want me to help you down there?

SPENCER (*Most definitely*)   I do *not*.

MRS. SCRANTON   Well, you don't have to bite my head off.
(*She slams the door and goes back to her work.* SPENCER *now picks up one of the boy's hands and kisses it warmly*)

SPENCER   Jesus Christ, Joker, I wanted you to live.
(*Now he takes his scalpel. It is the hardest thing he ever had to do in his life, and he has to steel himself to do it, but he severs the main arteries, feeling the pain of doing it to himself, and then drops to a chair, his perspiring face in his hands*)

Curtain

THE TINY CLOSET

*

* *

The scene is a boarding-rooming house somewhere in a Midwestern city. On stage we see the big living room of the house, which is Victorian in design, with ornate woodwork and high ceiling. The furnishings, too, are Victorian. An ornate wooden stairway is at the right, and the outside entrance is down right. As the curtain goes up, MR. NEWBOLD *is seen coming down the stairs. He is a man of about fifty, a large man and rather nice-looking. He is always impeccably dressed in the most conservative clothes, a dark blue suit, white shirt, modest tie, a high shine on his black shoes, and his thinning hair carefully combed. He is the sort of man who takes great pride in his grooming. Something now seems to be bothering him. When he gets to the bottom of the stairs, he stops a moment and thinks. Then he calls his landlady.*

MR. NEWBOLD Mrs. Crosby! (*No response*) Mrs. Crosby!

MRS. CROSBY (*Coming from the kitchen*) Yes, Mr. Newbold. I was just straightening up after breakfast. I'm afraid none of the guests like the new bacon I got. It's just as expensive as the other bacon I was serving. On my word it is. Every bit. I didn't buy it to bring down expenses. Not at all. It's *fine bacon*. Hickory smoked. Only it's the kind you slice yourself. That's

189

why I got it. You can cut yourself a good thick slice of bacon that you can really get your teeth into, instead of that other stuff that shrivels up like tissue paper . . . (*She is the sort of woman who continues talking until someone stops her*)

MR. NEWBOLD   Mrs. Crosby . . .

MRS. CROSBY   Yes, Mr. Newbold!

MR. NEWBOLD   Mrs. Crosby, you remember before I moved in I specified that no one was to enter my closet . . .

MRS. CROSBY   Indeed I remember, Mr. Newbold. And I told you you could have your own lock on the closet, like you asked me. No one around here has any keys to your closet but *you,* Mr. Newbold . . .

MR. NEWBOLD   Nevertheless, Mrs. Crosby . . .

MR. CROSBY   . . . and I told the colored woman, "Elsie, you're not to enter Mr. Newbold's closet. Mr. Newbold," I told her, "is a perfectly orderly gentleman who is perfectly capable of keeping his own closet, and you're not to bother it." I gave her strict orders, Mr. Newbold.

MR. NEWBOLD   Nevertheless, Mrs. Crosby . . .

MRS. CROSBY   And as for me, goodness, I never go near the rooms. I got enough on my hands downstairs without bothering about the upstairs. I leave all that to Elsie. I don't suppose I been upstairs now in almost . . .

MR. NEWBOLD   Mrs. Crosby, a closet is a very small space. That's all I ask in this life. That's all I ask, just that tiny closet to call my own, my very own.

MRS. CROSBY   I quite understand, Mr. Newbold. We all have to have some place that's private to us, where we don't invite the world to see. I quite understand.

MR. NEWBOLD   But someone has been monkeying with the lock on the door, Mrs. Crosby.

MRS. CROSBY   (*Shocked*)   You don't say!

MR. NEWBOLD   I *do* say, Mrs. Crosby. Someone has been monkeying with that expensive Yale lock I had put on the door.

MRS. CROSBY   Do you suppose someone coulda got up there when no one was around and . . .

MR. NEWBOLD   I'm sure I don't know, but I won't stand for anyone's monkeying with that lock, Mrs. Crosby. That room, while I rent it, is my private property, and I gave strict instructions that no one was to go near the closet, and I expect my orders to be respected.

MRS. CROSBY   Of course, Mr. Newbold, you're my favorite of all the roomers. Oh, I wish they was all like you. You keep your room spotless, and you're always so correct around the house. My, you're a model guest. You really are. You should open up a class out here at that night school they have for adults and teach 'em how to behave in their rooming houses. The landladies in this town would get together and thank you.

MR. NEWBOLD   Thank you, Mrs. Crosby. Nevertheless, I must repeat that that closet is my personal property. There is nothing inside I am ashamed of. It's not that. It's only that I have *some* place, just some little place, that's completely private. That no one has access to. That's all I ask, Mrs. Crosby.

MRS. CROSBY   And I quite understand, Mr. Newbold.

MR. NEWBOLD   Very well. As long as that is clearly understood, I hope I'll not have to bring the subject up again, Mrs. Crosby.

MRS. CROSBY   I'll tell Elsie again, Mr. Newbold. I'll give special emphasis that no one is to go near that closet.

MR. NEWBOLD   Thank you, Mrs. Crosby. (*Looks at his watch*) Goodness! I mustn't dally another minute.

MRS. CROSBY   Did you see Mrs. Hergesheimer in the store yesterday, Mr. Newbold?

MR. NEWBOLD   Mrs. Hergesheimer? Oh yes, I believe I did.

MRS. CROSBY   She called me yesterday and told me she seen you. "Whata fine man that Mr. Newbold is!" she says. "You're a lucky woman, Mrs. Crosby, to have such a fine guest. All I got in my house is a lota old-maid school teachers and I'm always cleanin' up after 'em." That's what she says. "Oh, men are much tidier than women, I told her." I kept school teachers once and they was always in the bathroom, curling their hair in there or giving themselves shampoos, or shaving their legs on my nice bedspreads. *Mr.* Crosby was alive then, and it almost drove him crazy. He never could get to the bathroom when he wanted to, because of them school teachers.

MR. NEWBOLD   Good day, Mrs. Crosby.
(*He puts on his hat and goes out the door*)

MRS. CROSBY   Good day, Mr. Newbold! (*Calling to him outside the door*) You be here for dinner tonight, won't you?

MR. NEWBOLD (*Off*)   I intend to be.

MRS. CROSBY (*Closing the door*)   Good day, Mr. Newbold. (*Now she comes back inside the room. Curiosity
is about to kill her. She is childishly excited. She goes
back to the door and peers out to make sure that* MR.
NEWBOLD *is on his way. Then she comes back and
goes to the telephone, dialing her number*) Mrs. Hergesheimer? Have you got a minute? He's just left.
"You're not to go into my room," he says to me again,
for the two-hundredth time. "Someone's been playing
with the lock on my door and you're not to go near that
closet," he says, like it was his house and he was order-
ing me about. Can you beat it? Now what do you suppose he's got hid away in that closet? (*She listens
awhile*) No, I can't think he'd be a Communist, Mrs.
Hergesheimer. Of course, he *might* be. You never can
tell. But I don't think that's it, somehow. (*She listens
again*) Love letters? But why would he need a whole
closet for his love letters, if he's got any. Besides, I
don't think he's the type of man that has love letters.
(*She listens*) It's certainly a mystery. I confess, it's
certainly a mystery. What would *you* do, Mrs. Hergesheimer? (*A pause*) You would? Well, hurry over, why
don't you, and we'll try again. Hurry! (*She hangs up,
then calls to the kitchen*) Elsie, you're not to go upstairs for a while. Mrs. Hergesheimer is comin' over
and she and I have some things we wanta do up there,
so you're to keep busy with the washin'. Understand?

ELSIE (*Off*)   Yes, Mrs. Crosby.

(*Now* MRS. CROSBY *spends a few minutes of nervous
activity. Her conscience bothers her some, but primar-
ily she is afraid of being caught. She looks out the door
again, then out of each window, then calls out to the
kitchen again*)

MRS. CROSBY Remember, Elsie, you're not to bother me for a while. I'll let you know when I want you, Elsie. You're to stay out there till I call you.

(*Now* MRS. HERGESHEIMER *hurries into the house*)

MRS. HERGESHEIMER I think you've got every *right*, Mrs. Crosby. Every right.

MRS. CROSBY That's what I've been telling myself, Mrs. Hergesheimer. I've got every *right*. For all I know, I may be harboring a *spy*, or a criminal, or a lunatic. What's he got in that closet that he don't want anyone to see? Can you tell me? It must be something he's ashamed of, or he wouldn't mind if anyone saw. Isn't that what you say? And if it's something he's ashamed of, I think we should find out what it is. You can't tell, he might have a bomb in there he meant to destroy us with. I'm not gonna set idly by while someone is plotting something, Mrs. Hergesheimer. I pride myself, I'm a real American, and I say, if anyone's got any secrets he wants to keep hid, let 'em come out into the open and declare himself. Mr. Newbold has always seemed like a fine man, and I got nothin' against him personally, and he's the best roomer I ever had, keeps his room spotless. Elsie don't have to do anything but make the bed. And I appreciate that, but if you ask me, it's kinda unnatural for a man to be so tidy. Isn't that what you say? There's been something suspicious about him from the very first.

MRS. HERGESHEIMER I made a point of talking to him when I was shopping in Baumgarden's yesterday. My, he struts around that floor. You'd think he was president instead of a floorwalker. I asked him where they kept the artificial flowers. I knew, but I just wanted to see if he'd recognize me. He smiled and made a lordly gesture with his hand, showin' me the way. You'd have thought he was the King of Persia with all his fine manners.

MRS. CROSBY   He belongs to the Lions' Club. Do you think he'd be a Communist and still belong to the Lions' Club?

MRS. HERGESHEIMER   You can't tell. Lots of them join clubs like that just as a cover-up. That school teacher I got—she's a Red and I know it. Brings home all kinds of books to read. Yes. Dangerous books. But she goes to church every Sunday morning, just as big as you please, just to pretend she's *not* a Red.

MRS. CROSBY   Forevermore!

MRS. HERGESHEIMER   I think you've got every right to go into that closet, Mrs. Crosby.

MRS. CROSBY   Yes, I think so, too. Well . . . Well, you come with me.

MRS. HERGESHEIMER   Oh, Mrs. Crosby, honey, I don't think it's right for me to do it. I'll stay down here and see that Elsie doesn't bother you.

MRS. CROSBY   I'm not going to do it if you don't come with me.

MRS. HERGESHEIMER   Well . . .

MRS. CROSBY   After all, you've been just as curious about this as I've been, and I think you owe it to me to come along.

MRS. HERGESHEIMER   Well, if that's the way you feel about it, Mrs. Crosby, I'll come along. After all, it's not as though we were doing anything criminal.

MRS. CROSBY   Indeed it's not. Come on then.
(*She starts toward the stairs, taking a final look toward the kitchen to make sure that Elsie is occupied*)

MRS. HERGESHEIMER (*Following with some trepidation*)
Oh dear, I hope he doesn't find out.

MRS. CROSBY   We can get that lock off this time without
making any more scratches than we made yesterday.
He won't notice.

MRS. HERGESHEIMER   Oh, I bet he does. He's got a
sharp eye.

MRS. CROSBY   Well, I don't care if he does. I've got a
right to see what's in that closet.

MRS. HERGESHEIMER   Yes . . . Well . . . go on, Mrs.
Crosby. I'm right behind you. (*Slowly, cautiously, the
two women go up the stairs together. The stage is
empty for a few moments, then* ELSIE *comes in from
the kitchen, looks up the stairs with curiosity. Then,
as though the behavior of the two women was too
much for her to understand, she shrugs her shoulders,
laughs gently, and returns to kitchen. The stage is
empty again for a few moments. Then, slowly, the front
door opens and* MR. NEWBOLD *returns inside the house.
He has suspected the two women to do exactly what
they're doing. He is very nervous. His heart is pounding. He starts up the stairs and then comes down again.
He can't seem to get the courage to confront the
women. The starch he showed earlier in the play has
dissolved. He is perspiring heavily and twisting his
hands in fear and excitement. In a few moments we
hear the women on their way downstairs.* MR. NEW-
BOLD *hurriedly finds a closet to hide in. The two
women come down the stairs slowly, in awed silence.*
MRS. CROSBY *carries a woman's hat, a large hat, the
kind a graceful lady might wear to a garden party. It
is quite a lovely hat, in a light pastel color with great
flowers on its limber brim and sleek satin ribbons. They*

come forward together, MRS. CROSBY *holding the hat, both of them studying it with bafflement*) Hats! Dozens of hats!

MRS. CROSBY   I can't believe it.

MRS. HERGESHEIMER   He must have brought them home from the store, don't you think?

MRS. CROSBY   But there was all that sewing equipment on a shelf.

MRS. HERGESHEIMER   But no man could make hats as lovely as these.

MRS. CROSBY   I don't know. There's something kinda unusual about Mr. Newbold. I think he might have made them. I . . . I know he did. (*Suddenly recalls a clue*) I remember now how he was always looking through the fashion magazines. Sometimes he'd take them up to his room. He'd *study* them. I always wondered why.

MRS. HERGESHEIMER   But why would he stay up in his room making hats? And then keep them locked in his closet?

MRS. CROSBY   He . . . he's just peculiar. That's all. He's just peculiar. I thought so, the first time I saw the man. He's too prim for a man. He's too tidy the way he keeps his room. It's just not natural.

MRS. HERGESHEIMER   Oh, I wish now we hadn't looked.

MRS. CROSBY   I had a perfect right.

MRS. HERGESHEIMER   I know, but . . .

MRS. CROSBY   Why, I think he's the most peculiar man I ever heard of. Why, I'd rather be harboring a Communist.

MRS. HERGESHEIMER   Oh, Mrs. Crosby, don't say that.

MRS. CROSBY   I would. I'd rather be harboring a Communist than a man who makes hats.

MRS. HERGESHEIMER   Why, there's nothing wrong with making hats. I don't see anything wrong with it. Why, lots of men make hats. Some of the finest designers there are are men. Why, of course.

MRS. CROSBY   But he kept them locked in his closet. He was ashamed of them. He was.

MRS. HERGESHEIMER   Maybe it's just a hobby with him. Some men knit, you know, because it helps their nerves.

MRS. CROSBY   I'm going to ask him to leave.

MRS. HERGESHEIMER   Oh no, Mrs. Crosby. Don't do that.

MRS. CROSBY   I am. I'm going to ask him to leave. And I'm going to call the store he works at and tell them what kind of a freak they have working for them. Indeed I am.

MRS. HERGESHEIMER   Oh, I wouldn't do that. It's not against the law for a man to make hats. He hasn't done anything really wrong.

MRS. CROSBY   Why, a man who'd make hats and lock them up in his closet, there's no telling what kind of a person he is. He might do any kind of dangerous, crazy thing.

MRS. HERGESHEIMER   Oh, I don't think so, Mrs. Crosby. Really I don't.

MRS. CROSBY   I'd rather he was a Communist. At least you know what a Communist is up to. But a man that makes hats? What can you tell about such a creature?

MRS. HERGESHEIMER   I wouldn't give it another thought if I was you.

MRS. CROSBY   Well, I guess it takes all kinds of people to make a world.

MRS. HERGESHEIMER   Of course. That's the way to look at it.

MRS. CROSBY   Hats! Hats! Hats! With flowers on them.

MRS. HERGESHEIMER   I must run along now.

MRS. CROSBY   Hats!

MRS. HERGESHEIMER   Goodness, I hope he never finds out.

MRS. CROSBY   I don't care if he does. Just let him try to scold me, in that superior way of his. (*Imitating* MR. NEWBOLD) "Mrs. Crosby, someone's been tampering with the lock on my closet. I demand privacy, Mrs. Crosby. That's all I ask is just one tiny closet to call my own. That's all I ask." Hmm. I'll have an answer for him. "What in God's name does a grown-up man like you mean by making hats, Mr. Newbold? Shame!" That's what I'll tell him. And he won't act so superior then.

(MRS. HERGESHEIMER *flutters out of the house as though wanting to avoid further involvement.* MRS. CROSBY *studies the hat once more, then takes it to the mirror and tries it on, looking at herself in it, assuming a variety of poses with the hat, at times mocking its elegance with a feeling of low burlesque. Then she tosses it on a chair and goes to the kitchen. After a few moments,* MR. NEWBOLD *comes out of the closet in which he has been hiding. He is a shattered man. All of his pride, his erect posture, his air of authority are gone. He has become a shy and frightened young girl. Lovingly, he picks up the hat and carries it to the mirror where he puts it on, looking at himself. He strikes one or two poses in an effort to create some image of beauty, but he does not succeed. The image has been destroyed for him. He drops the hat onto a chair, then himself falls onto the sofa and cries like a hopeless child)*

Curtain

*
MEMORY
OF SUMMER
* *

*The time is late September, and the scene is the beach
of a now-desolate resort. The sea presumably is at the left
of the stage, and a wall, about shoulder-high, lines the
back. Powerful waves crack against the shore. At the
right are a few shops or stands that were full of noisy
activity all summer, but now are boarded up, and an
occasional wind goes whistling through their emptiness,
sending the last bits of summer refuse (paper napkins,
candy wrappers, etc.) scattering over the sand. It is a
chilly day and the atmosphere is damp and gray.* VIOLA
*comes through a gate in the wall at the back. She is a
slim woman in her forties, with a delicate prettiness.
There is a fragile smile on her face, a rather unrealistic
smile that exists for itself. She wears an elegant cloak
over her swimsuit and carries a large towel. Her feet are
in sandals. She walks to the left of the stage, slowly, her
eyes looking out at the sea. Then in the background can
be heard the voice of the old housekeeper,* ALICE.

ALICE (*A worried voice, off*)   Miss Viola! Miss Viola!

VIOLA (*Lightly*)   You needn't worry about me, Alice.
(ALICE *comes through the gate. She is a woman in her
sixties. She is concerned and fretful*)

ALICE   Oh, Miss Viola, *do* come back to the cottage!
It's late September and there's a chill in the air. You
shouldn't be going for a swim.

VIOLA   Why, it's a splendid day, Alice. And you know how I love the water. Sometimes the water is very warm on a day like this. Really it is. Why, this is a perfect day for a swim.

ALICE   Miss Viola, the summer's over . . .

VIOLA   Nonsense, Alice.

ALICE   The summer's long over, Miss Viola, and we should be returning home.

VIOLA   (*Blandly*)   Home?

ALICE   You have a husband and a fine home waiting for you in Saint Louis, Miss Viola. Why don't you come back to the cottage with me now, and we'll make our reservations and start our packing.

VIOLA   (*A flicker of anguish on her face*)   It's my holiday, Alice.

ALICE   The holiday's over, Miss Viola. Can't I make you see? Can't you understand?

VIOLA   (*Gayly*)   My holiday isn't over. Why, I feel that it's just begun. I know the sky is a little dark now, but the water is still . . . quite warm. And you know how I love the sea. Every morning I must have my dip. It's the first thing I think of when I awaken: I'll have my breakfast, I tell myself, and then I'll hurry to the beach, where all the young people are laughing and playing and . . . (*She catches herself*)

ALICE   (*Cautiously*)   Miss Viola . . . there aren't any young people here now. There's no one here now.

VIOLA   (*Forcing a little laugh*)   They're all sissies. They're afraid of the water, just because the sun is under. Don't they know they can't expect every day to be sunny and bright?

ALICE   Look, Miss Viola, the shops are all boarded up.
The young lifeguards have all gone back to school. All
the venders are gone, too. See? There's none of them
around. You're all alone now. There's no one left but
the Beach Patrol, and I'll have to call them if you go
in the water, Miss Viola. I'll *have* to.

VIOLA *(Laughing)*   Dear Alice! You sounded then just
like you did when I was a child, and you had to call
me in from play.

ALICE   I wish I could reason with you, Miss Viola.

VIOLA   You hurry back to the cottage, Alice. I want you
to press my white piqué for me. I'm dining at the
inn . . .

ALICE *(Trying to protest)*   Miss Viola . . .

VIOLA   I'll be dining at the inn, and the inn will be full
of young people, beautiful young people, dancing, and
they mustn't point at me for looking dowdy and old.
You don't want your Viola to be pointed at and
scoffed at, do you, Alice? I want to look *young* for
them, Alice. And I'll dance with the young men, too.
And I'll laugh for them. And I'll tell my naughty little
stories for them, my naughty-nice stories, to amuse
them. For they mustn't think I am a prude. And I'll
dance and laugh with them, while the little orchestra is
playing those sweet, *sweet* melodies; and I'll come
home long after midnight, simply exhausted, and fall
into my lovely bed and let you cover me with soft, soft
blankets . . .

ALICE   Miss Viola, there's no one at the inn. The orchestra played its last dance on Labor Day.

VIOLA (*Gayly*) . . . and put out my blue satin slippers
and my nicest lingerie! And if the night air is a little
chilly, I'll wear my furs . . .
(*She goes running off into the water*)

ALICE (*Frantically calling*)   Miss Viola! Miss Viola!
(*Suddenly there is the shrill sound of a whistle. Then
a young* COAST GUARD *scales the wall and lands grace-
fully on his feet. He is a young man of almost god-like
handsomeness, still bronzed from the summer sun. He
wears a beach helmet and the summer fatigues uniform
of the Coast Guard*)

COAST GUARD (*To Alice*)   Is the lady *loco?*

ALICE   I wish someone could stop her.

COAST GUARD   She's been here every day. We saw her
from the lookout. We're supposed to keep people off
the beach after Labor Day, but we didn't want to say
anything, as long as the weather was O.K. and the sea
was smooth.

ALICE   I couldn't stop her.

COAST GUARD (*Blows his whistle and calls after* VIOLA)
You gotta come in! You gotta come in! (*To* ALICE) She
a good swimmer?

ALICE   Yes. She loves to swim. She's a very good swimmer.

COAST GUARD   The water's rough today and there's a stiff
undercurrent. It's cold, too.

ALICE   I'm going back to the cottage and call her doctor.
He told me to call him if she acted this way. He doesn't
know what to do with the dear child.

COAST GUARD (*Using hands as a megaphone*)   You gotta
come in! You gotta come in!

ALICE (*Handing him the beach blanket*)   Wrap her up
in this. And here's a little brandy I brought along for
her. (*Hands him a flask*) She likes it and I thought it'd
warm her. I'm going back to the cottage and call her
doctor.
(*She hurries off*)

COAST GUARD (*Walking to the water. Obviously* VIOLA
has started back. He calls to her) What *are* you, an
Eskimo? (*He waits*) The water's in the sixties. We
can't let anyone go in the water this time of year. (*He
still waits, holding up the blanket for her*) Come on,
let me wrap this around you.
(VIOLA *comes out of the water, seeking her blanket*)

VIOLA   I had a lovely swim. Really, the water was sur-
prisingly warm. I had a lovely swim.
(*She dries herself hurriedly*)

COAST GUARD   We can't let you go in any more, lady.
You gotta stop these little beach parties, at least until
next season.

VIOLA   Next season?

COAST GUARD (*Wrapping the blanket around her*)   Yah.
This one's over.

VIOLA   Thank you, young man, for your attentions.

COAST GUARD   The next time you go in, I'll have to come
in and get you.

VIOLA   You will?

COAST GUARD   Yes, ma'am. And I wouldn't like that at
all.

VIOLA   But that's absurd. The sea is quite public. Certainly I have the right to go for my usual morning dip
without making myself the cause of such concern.

COAST GUARD   Sorry, lady, but I can't let you go in any more.

VIOLA   I must say, I appreciate your thoughtfulness and concern. It's most gallant of you, but . . .

COAST GUARD   It's not gallant, lady. It's just my orders.

VIOLA   Oh!

COAST GUARD   I should have stopped you before this. If you were to drown, I'd get sent to the brig for not doing my duty.

VIOLA   I see. Well, I shouldn't wish to cause anyone trouble. (*She looks around nervously*) Did Alice leave some brandy for me?

COAST GUARD   (*Handing her the flask*)   Here, ma'am.

VIOLA   Thank you. (*Takes a swallow*) I wish I could offer *you* some.

COAST GUARD   I never drink on duty, ma'am.

VIOLA   Oh!

COAST GUARD   Thank you, just the same.

VIOLA   If you'd care to come by the cottage sometime, I'd gladly offer you a drink, when you were not on duty.

COAST GUARD   Thank you, ma'am. I very seldom go out here. When I'm off duty, I go into town.

VIOLA   Now, you probably are thinking I'm one of those horrid old women who go around flirting with handsome young men. Of course that's what you're thinking!

COAST GUARD   No, ma'am, I . . .

VIOLA   I insist on your understanding that where I come
from, I should have been considered most ungracious
if I hadn't offered some little sign of hospitality to you
. . . after your kindness.

COAST GUARD   Thank you, just the same.

VIOLA   Now where did Alice go?

COAST GUARD   Your maid returned to the cottage,
ma'am.

VIOLA   Did she? And left you to stay and look after me?

COAST GUARD   Yes, ma'am, I . . .

VIOLA   Now, I should have brought my beach basket
along. I had such gay times all summer long. Every
day I brought a huge basket to the beach with me, full
of the most delicious goodies, and always with a great
Thermos full of daiquiris; and I always brought along
a little radio, too, to provide cheerful music for the
day. I held court, one might say, on the beach. I was
hostess all day long to the young people.

COAST GUARD   I have to be getting back to the lookout,
ma'am.

VIOLA   You . . . are a handsome young man, aren't
you?

COAST GUARD   Am I? Thank you, ma'am.

VIOLA   Now you mustn't think I'm being fresh again.
You *don't,* do you?

COAST GUARD   No, ma'am, I . . .

VIOLA   I see no reason at all why I shouldn't say it. I
admire a handsome young man, and men have never
hesitated to tell me I was pretty, so I think it only fair
in return for me to tell you that you're *very* handsome.

COAST GUARD (*More embarrassed*)   Thank you.

VIOLA   From the water, I saw you scaling the wall after you had blown your rude whistle at me, and you were like a god.

COAST GUARD   A god?

VIOLA   Yes, like an angry sea god, scaling walls to save a disobedient naiad.

COAST GUARD   Oh.

VIOLA   A naiad is a water nymph. In Greek mythology.

COAST GUARD   Yes, ma'am.

VIOLA   A *nymph* to the Greeks was something entirely different from what the term implies today.

COAST GUARD   I . . . I don't know much about such things. (VIOLA *shivers*) You better get back to your cottage, ma'am, and get warm.

VIOLA   Ah, but I *can't* leave my glorious beach.

COAST GUARD   You're cold, ma'am. You're shivering and your hands are trembling.

VIOLA (*Looking at him blankly*)   Are they?

COAST GUARD   You need something to warm you.

VIOLA   I do?

ALICE (*Off, calling*)   Miss Viola! Miss Viola!!

COAST GUARD   Here comes your maid, ma'am. I'll run along.
(*He runs fleetly off*)

VIOLA (*Following a few steps after him, calling*)   Young man! Young man!
(*Politely he returns*)

COAST GUARD   Yes, ma'am?

VIOLA (*Fumblingly*) I . . . I feel I must thank you for looking after me.

COAST GUARD That's all right, ma'am. Like I said, I was only carrying out orders.

VIOLA It's very courteous of you to refuse my thanks, but, nevertheless, you have behaved with the most courageous thoughtfulness and . . . and valor and . . .

COAST GUARD (*Quite puzzled by her*) It was nothing, ma'am.

VIOLA (*Taking his hand*) Nevertheless . . . I wish to thank you from the bottom of my heart . . .

ALICE (*Hurrying on*) Miss Viola, you must come back to the cottage now. Your doctor's coming.

VIOLA The young man says I need something to make me warm, Alice.
(*She laughs*)

ALICE Of course you do. (*Nodding to the* COAST GUARD) I'll take her home now.

COAST GUARD Good day!
(*He runs off*)

VIOLA (*Hovering in Alice's arms*) The young man said I needed something to make me warm.

ALICE There's a log fire going in the cabin. I'll have a hot tub ready for you and then a cup of broth. Your doctor insists that you go into the city. He's going to take you to see another doctor, Miss Viola. Now be reasonable.

VIOLA (*In a faraway voice, looking about her*) Where are all the young people today, Alice?

ALICE They're gone.

VIOLA   Gone?

ALICE   Yes, dear! They've all gone back to school.

VIOLA   But, this is where the young people belong, on a sunny beach, surrounded by clear blue water and splashing waves . . . laughing and playing in the sand.

ALICE   The season's over, Miss Viola.

VIOLA   And you must get out my white piqué for me to wear to the inn tonight, Alice.

ALICE   But your doctor's coming, Miss Viola. Here, dear, keep the blanket around you. You're shivering.

VIOLA   The young man said I needed something to keep me warm.

ALICE   (*Leading her off*)   Yes, dear. We'll go back to the cottage and hug the cozy fire until your doctor comes.

VIOLA   And tonight I must look my best for the young people. I shall delight them with my stories, and I shall dance more gayly than any of them. And I shall wear my blue satin slippers, and my lovely furs, if the night air is at all chilly . . .

ALICE   Yes, Miss Viola.

VIOLA   (*As they go off,* ALICE *hugs her close to her*) And tomorrow will be a lovely day at the beach. The bright sun will beat down on us and warm us through and through, but we can always run into the breakers and have a quick, cool dip to refresh us, can't we? And all the beautiful young people will be laughing and playing together in the sand . . .

Curtain

BUS RILEY'S
BACK IN TOWN

The scene of the play is the Fiesta Room of the Hotel Boomerang in a small town in middle Texas. The Fiesta Room is only the bar of the hotel, and as a bar not a very satisfactory one, being permitted to sell only beer. But the décor pretends, at least, to an air of festivity, with symbols of primitive Mexican culture. Mexican hats and serapes hang on the wall, there is a big poster of a bullfight, and the doors to the toilets are marked, one Señora, the other Señor. But there is not much festivity in the Fiesta Room at present. Only one customer is in view, a SALESMAN, *sitting at the bar, drinking a glass of beer and reading an evening paper.* HOWIE, *the bar-tender, an easygoing man of middle age, stays behind the bar, not even pretending to keep busy.*

SALESMAN   Used t'be I'd come into this town and sell maybe five thousand dollars' worth a merchandise in one day.

HOWIE   Bet ya don't do that now, do you?

SALESMAN   No. I'm doin' good now if I make my expenses in this town. I ain't kiddin'.

HOWIE   Yah. Things ain't what they used to be around here. That drought didn't help us any.

SALESMAN   Yah. That drought was bad.

215

HOWIE   But this little town really had it once.

SALESMAN   It sure did. (*He looks around the room*)
This all the customers ya got, Howie?

HOWIE   It's early in the week. We don't do enough
business to stay open, except on Friday and Saturday
nights. There's always a crowd in here then.

SALESMAN   Things have sure changed. They sure have.

HOWIE   The business we do on weekends has to carry
us through the week. It's the hotel's worry. Not mine.
They wanta keep the room open just for the looks of
things. When we have a losing week, I guess they
make up for it with the dining room. The dining room
does a pretty good business.

SALESMAN   Yah. It's about the only place in town you
can get decent food. All you can get in these lunch
stands around here is greaser food—chili and tamales.
I can't eat it.
(*Now a young girl comes running into the room from
the outside. She is* JACKIE LOOMIS, *a quite pretty girl
of twenty-three or twenty-four, wearing a simple summer wash frock, spectator pumps and no stockings.
There is something taut about her, a breathlessness
that makes her seem to live every moment as though
it were a crisis. She runs to the bar excitedly and
speaks to* HOWIE)

JACKIE   (*In a somewhat private voice*)   Howie, is it
true Bus Riley's in town?

HOWIE   Yes, Jackie. At least, he was in town a day or
so ago. His father, you know, has been real sick, and
Bus had to come home to give him blood transfusions.
Bus has been spending most of his time at the hospital,
they say.

JACKIE   Has he been in here, Howie?

HOWIE   Yes, a few times. Usually comes in at night and has a few beers.

JACKIE   What's he like now, Howie?

HOWIE   Like? Well, I . . . uh . . .

JACKIE   Is he still a *god?*

HOWIE   (*Chuckles*)   Well, I don't know I'd say he was a *god.* He looked pretty much like the same old Bus to me. The only difference I could see was he was wearing a sailor suit.

JACKIE   I've just *got* to see him, Howie. I've just *got* to.

HOWIE   (*At a loss for what to say*)   Well, Jackie, I . . .

JACKIE   Don't tell anyone, Howie. Please don't tell anyone I asked about him. Will you promise?

HOWIE   No. I won't tell, Jackie.

JACKIE   Is he staying at home, do you know, Howie?

HOWIE   As far as I know, Jackie.

JACKIE   (*Digs into her purse for a piece of change*) Give me a dime, Howie.

HOWIE   You bet, Jackie.
(*She takes the dime from him and hurries into the telephone booth in a corner*)

SALESMAN   (*An observant man*)   That was Del Loomis's daughter, wasn't it?

HOWIE   Yep!

SALESMAN   How is old Del these days?

HOWIE   The same, I guess. No one ever sees him.

SALESMAN Dead drunk, I suppose.

HOWIE I suppose. They keep a nurse with him mosta the time.

SALESMAN Just think. He built this hotel, din he?

HOWIE Built mosta the buildings in town.

SALESMAN And now, they tell me, he don't have a nickel.

HOWIE Dead drunk. Dead broke. Poor old Del.

SALESMAN Yah. Well, he had it once, though.

HOWIE Yah. Del had millions.

SALESMAN Lived like a lord.

HOWIE Had a whole fleet of automobiles, two ranches, swimming pool, fifty servants, several airplanes. Kept a yacht down in the Gulf.

SALESMAN Yah. It just don't seem possible that a man can have as much as old Del did and then lose it.

HOWIE Del Loomis just about made this town. He ran things here pretty much the way he wanted 'em. We all kowtowed to him.

SALESMAN It was a one-man town.

HOWIE Yah! When Del had it, all of us here were prosperous, working in his oil fields and at the ranches. He kept things humming. Then he lost it, and so did the rest of us. I guess we all owe a lot to Del, and he was a likable man, too, in a way. I mean he was always friendly when he met you on the street. But I guess all that money and all that power kinda went to his head. He was actin' kinda crazy around here, like he was Nero or one of those Roman emperors.

SALESMAN   Yah. I think Del was goin' off his rocker. That's what I think. (*He nods in the direction of* JACKIE, *who is still in the telephone booth*) That the daughter there was all the talk about? (HOWIE *nods a little reluctantly*) In love with some fellow Del didn't want her to marry, wasn't she?

HOWIE   That's it. The story got in all the papers. It all happened five or six years ago.

SALESMAN   This is the first time I ever saw her. She sure is a looker.

HOWIE   Del was crazy about her. He acted to me like he was jealous of the boy and in love with her him- self.
(*Two young people come in:* RALPH *and* BERNICE HENRY, *a married couple, friends of* JACKIE. *A little mystified, they are looking for her*)

BERNICE   (*To* HOWIE)   Did Jackie come in here?

HOWIE   (*Nodding to the telephone booth*)   In there, Bernice.

BERNICE   Oh.
(JACKIE, *seeing* BERNICE *and* RALPH, *hurries out of the booth, a little embarrassed with a feeling of hav- ing been caught*)

JACKIE   Oh, I was just calling home, Bee. I . . . I just remembered that Daddy asked me to. He said maybe he'd want me to bring something home from town.

BERNICE   (*A little miffed*)   Well, you might have told us. Ralph and I were looking all over for you after the movie let out. You made off in such a hurry. I thought we'd come over here together. We always do.

JACKIE   I . . . I'm sorry, Bee.

RALPH   What's the difference? Let's sit down and have a beer. (*He leads* BERNICE *to a booth on the side of the room opposite the bar, calling to* HOWIE *on the way*) Three beers, Howie!

BERNICE (*Still a little peeved at* JACKIE)   Maybe you want to get rid of Ralph and me.

JACKIE   No, Bee. Honest! It's just that I remembered suddenly that I'd promised Daddy to call. Honest!

BERNICE (*Looking at her a little dubiously*)   Well, I don't see why you had to go running off that way, without even saying a word.
(*She sits next to* RALPH *in the booth. Then* JACKIE *joins them, sitting opposite them*)

RALPH (*To* BERNICE)   It doesn't make any difference, Mama. We're not Jackie's guardians, or anything.
(HOWIE *goes over and sets down three beers for them*)

BERNICE   Oh, did you order beer for me? I'm not sure I want it. It makes me feel so logy in hot weather.

HOWIE   Want me to take it back?

BERNICE   No. I'll drink it. Darn! I wish you could order a Tom Collins in this town, or a gin and tonic. (HOWIE *returns to the bar*) Lord, that was a putrid movie. Now, when they try to make an ancient Egyptian princess out of Lana Turner, I just don't believe it. I don't care what you say, I don't believe it. She's about as Egyptian as our Scotty. Did you like the picture, Jackie?

JACKIE   I . . . I didn't pay much attention to it.

BERNICE   Jackie, you're so nervous these days, I don't know what to make of you.

JACKIE   I'm not usually, Bee. It's just tonight. I . . . I guess I *am* a little nervous tonight.

BERNICE   What about?

JACKIE   I . . . I don't know, Bee. Just nervous. That's all.

BERNICE   Now, Jackie honey, you wanta look after yourself, and when you find yourself getting nervous, go home and relax. Take it easy. Isn't that what you say, Ralph?

RALPH   Sure. Take it easy. That's my motto.

JACKIE   (*A little annoyed by* BERNICE'S *assumed authority*)   It's nothing to get worried about, Bee.

BERNICE   Did you like the movie, Ralph?

RALPH   I liked the photography. The color was pretty.

BERNICE   That's all you care about. The photography. I like a story that's *real,* that shows just how nasty people really are, and doesn't mince words about it.

RALPH   Can't a movie be real if it shows people being nice, too?

BERNICE   Maybe. But what's the point? I mean . . .

JACKIE   (*Suddenly jumping up from her seat*)   Pardon me a minute, kids, will you?

BERNICE   Oh . . . sure. (JACKIE *disappears into the door marked* Señora. BERNICE *watches her and now reports to* RALPH)   Do you know what she's going to do?

RALPH   Well, I take it for granted that when a girl pardons herself to go to the ladies' room, that she's going to do one of two things.

BERNICE (*Shaking her head wisely*)   Huh-uh. She's got
you fooled. I know what she's going to do. She's going
to take another of those pills.

RALPH   What pills?

BERNICE   Those sleeping pills she carries around with
her.

RALPH   Honey, you keep telling me she takes sleeping
pills, but if she does, why doesn't she ever go to
sleep?

BERNICE   Ralph, don't you know anything about these
things? She gets *high* on them, just like on liquor.
Honest. I bet anything she's taking a pill now and
just doesn't want us to know. You know why she
ditched us after the movie, don't you?

RALPH   I'm perfectly willing to believe that she had to
come over here to call her father.

BERNICE   Oh, you just don't know that girl. She came
over here in hopes of finding Bus Riley. And she
didn't want us to be around when she found him,
either. And that wasn't her father she was calling
when we came in. Huh-uh. She was calling Bus's
house. I bet anything.

RALPH   Well, what if she was? What's it to you?

BERNICE   It just so happens that Jackie Loomis is my
oldest, dearest friend. And I know all that she's been
through. I just want to spare her from going through
anything more . . . with that . . . that half-breed
Bus Riley.

RALPH   You think she still loves him?

BERNICE   Of course she does. She's been jumpy as a
cat, ever since she heard he was back. She's just been
dying to find some excuse to see him.

RALPH   After . . . everything that happened?

BERNICE   Of course.
(JACKIE *comes out of the ladies' room now. She seems quite merry. She lingers by the juke box, studying the selections, then going to the open door to see if* BUS *can be seen anywhere down the street*)

RALPH   My God, the guy's been in prison since then . . .

BERNICE   I know, but she's still crazy about him. Besides, it was her father sent Bus to prison. She knows that. (*She makes sure that* JACKIE *cannot overhear her*) Bus wasn't really guilty of anything. I mean, Jackie was as much to blame for getting pregnant as Bus was. Even if he was a year older. It was just old-man Loomis's way of getting revenge. He certainly wasn't going to let her marry Bus. Bus, half-Mexican, from the other side of the tracks.

RALPH   Bus was a pretty nice guy, though, honey. At least, when I knew him.

BERNICE   I'm not saying he wasn't. Still, he had a Mexican mother . . .

RALPH   But she's a very nice woman. I mean . . .

BERNICE   He lived out at the edge of town in that ugly little shanty full of kids.

RALPH   That's just because his old man wouldn't go to work.

BERNICE   All right. But what difference did that make to Del Loomis, when he was the richest man in middle Texas? He wouldn't have stood for Jackie marrying anyone like that. Why, Del Loomis was even trying to get Jackie married off to some European nobility.

RALPH   Del Loomis is a crackpot.

BERNICE   Maybe he is. But that doesn't keep the situation from being hopeless. It's just no good for Jackie to be getting excited all over again about Bus Riley. I don't know why he had to come back to town.

RALPH   His old man was about to die.

BERNICE   Yes, and you know why, don't you? Got stabbed in one of those Mexican joints he hangs out in, and lost almost all his blood.

RALPH   Well . . . you can't keep her from seeing Bus if she really wants to.

BERNICE   I can try.
(JACKIE *rejoins them at the booth;* BERNICE *becomes suddenly very silent*)

JACKIE   Oh, I don't want to go home tonight. I feel like I'd like to stay here until it closes. I don't want to go home.

BERNICE   Jackie, you can't stay here all alone. People would talk.

JACKIE   What difference would that make? People talk about me already.

BERNICE   That's not so, Jackie. You just imagine it.

JACKIE   (*With a quick little look at* BERNICE)   Do I?

BERNICE   Yes. Of course you do.

JACKIE   Well . . . maybe I do.

RALPH   I'm about ready for bed now, aren't you, Mother?

BERNICE   Yes, and we've got to relieve the baby-sitter.

JACKIE   Oh, let's not go yet. Please, let's not go yet.

BERNICE   Jackie, there's no point in sitting in this dump all evening. Come on over to our house if you want to. You can have a beer there. Or Ralph could fix you something stronger.

JACKIE   No thanks, Bee. You'll be busy looking after the children. I . . . I won't bother you.
(*Now* BUS RILEY *enters.* JACKIE *is aware of him the moment he comes through the door, and* BERNICE *sees a look come into her eyes.* BUS *is a very handsome young man of twenty-four or twenty-five, with sleek black hair and just a suggestion of Latin features and coloring. He wears his Navy whites with splendor. He calls to* HOWIE *as soon as he enters, not noticing the people in the booth*)

BUS   Draw me a beer, Howie! (*He strides to the bar*) Well, the Old Man's on the way to recovery now. I'm clearin' outa here in the morning.

HOWIE   Leavin' us so soon, Bus?

BUS   Yah. I've had enough of this town, forever.
(*He drinks his beer.* BERNICE *and* RALPH *get up from the booth*)

BERNICE   Let's go, Jackie.
(JACKIE *sits almost as though wounded by the sight and sound of* BUS)

JACKIE   Well, I . . .

BERNICE   You can't stay here, Jackie. You know you can't.

RALPH   Come along, Jackie old girl.

JACKIE   (*Reluctantly rising to her feet*) Well . . . if you say so . . . I . . .

RALPH (*To* BERNICE)   I'll pay the bill. You and Jackie go on out to the car.

BERNICE   O.K., honey.
(*Like a protecting angel,* BERNICE *hovers about* JACKIE, *getting her out of the bar before* BUS *sees her. At the bar,* RALPH *lays down a bill for* HOWIE *and gives* BUS *a hearty slap on the back*)

RALPH   Hello, Riley! Good to see you back.

BUS   Oh . . . Ralph Henry! Hi ya, Ralph?
(*They shake hands*)

RALPH   How's your father?

BUS   Gettin' along O.K. now. Doc says he's outa danger.

RALPH   Good. Glad to hear it. Well . . . nice to've seen you, Bus.

BUS   Yah . . . thanks, Ralph. (RALPH *goes out now.* BUS *is still trying to identify him*) Let's see. He married Bernice Cain, didn't he?

HOWIE   Right. She just went out . . . with an old friend of yours.

BUS   Who? You mean . . . ?

HOWIE   Yah. She was sitting right over there when you came in.

BUS   I'll be damned. Well . . . maybe it's a good thing I din see her. Know anywhere I could get a bottle of whiskey, Howie? I been cooped up in that hospital room for so long, I feel like celebratin' a little before I leave town.

HOWIE   You can't buy hard liquor in this county, Bus. You'll have to drive over to the next county, buy it there.

BUS   It was Del Loomis had that law passed, wasn't it?

HOWIE   I guess so.

BUS   He stayed home getting plastered, but thought the county should stay dry. That hypocrite son of a bitch! (*He shows intense hatred and anger*) Well, I'm goin' from here to Galveston. Things are a li'l different down there.

HOWIE   I hear things are wide open in Galveston.

SALESMAN   I hear they got gambling down there, and women.

BUS   You can get anything you want there. *Any*thing.

HOWIE   That where the Navy's been keepin' you all this time, Bus? Galveston?

BUS   Christ no! I've been everywhere there is to go. Around the world twice. I'm joining a new ship in Galveston. We sail for Hong Kong next week.

SALESMAN   (*His love of adventure stirred*)   Hong Kong!

BUS   Howie, what's the situation with girls in this town? The same as with whiskey?

HOWIE   (*Laughs and begins to ponder the question*) Well, let me think, Bus.

BUS   How about Melba Freeman? She still around?

HOWIE   No. Melba got herself a job in Dallas. Left here a few years ago.

BUS   Oh. That's too bad. Well . . . how 'bout Maxine Tucker? Where's she?

HOWIE   Oh, she's married, Bus. Married Lyn Overton. Remember him? They got two kids now. Happy as can be.

BUS Oh . . . that's great. Uh . . . whatever happened to Rosamund Skinner? There was a beauty.

HOWIE Rose got killed in a auto accident, Bus. About
a year ago. She and the boy she was with.

BUS Oh, gee, that's too bad.

HOWIE I'm afraid I can't think of anyone now, Bus.
The town's pretty quiet now.

BUS What the hell! I'll go down to the Mexican quarter.
I can pick up a chick there.

HOWIE I can give you a shot to go with that beer, if you
want it, Bus.

BUS *Do* I?

HOWIE I always keep a bottle back here to celebrate
with. And this is an occasion, you being home.
(*He pours out a jigger which* BUS *grabs instantly and
downs*)

BUS Thanks, Howie.

HOWIE How're things, Bus? I mean, on the level.

BUS O.K. *now,* Howie. I mean . . . Well, they kept
me in the cage for a year's all. I . . . I just don't
think about it any more. The minute I got out, I
made up my mind, I was never gonna think about it
again. So . . . I'm in the Navy now and life is great.
Sure. I get my kicks. Uh . . . Howie, how 'bout
another shot of that stuff? That's the first real drink
I've had since I got here; and man, I need it!

HOWIE Sure, Bus.
(*He pours another, which* BUS *immediately downs*)

BUS Thanks, Howie. You're a pal. If you could only
find me a girl, you'd be a *real* pal.

HOWIE   I might do that. (BUS *looks at him question-ingly*) Jackie's been asking me about you, Bus.

BUS   Has she?

HOWIE   She was calling you from here before Ralph and Bernice came in.

BUS   I guess I'd left the house.

HOWIE   I think she'd like to see you, Bus.

BUS   What's she like now, Howie?

HOWIE   Still the same sweet kid, Bus, and prettier'n ever.

BUS   Yah?

HOWIE   I bet she comes back here after she gets rid of Ralph and Bernice. I bet anything.

BUS   I'm not sure I'd know how to act around her now.

HOWIE   (*Looking out the front window*)   I was right. There she is now, pulling up at the curb. She let Ralph and Bernice take her home, then got into her own car and came right back. I told you she wanted to see you.

BUS   (*This is a troubled moment for* BUS, *not knowing whether he can face her or not*)   Howie, I don't know if I can . . .

HOWIE   What d'ya mean, Bus?

BUS   (*Making a start to get away*)   I'm heading out the back way. I can't see Jackie again.

HOWIE   (*Catching* BUS *at the end of the bar*)   Hold on, Bus. Hold on. She'll feel awful bad if you run off. (BUS *says nothing. He just stays where he is, his back to the door, his head down, dreading to face her.*

JACKIE *comes in. She is a little hesitant, a little un-
certain of her welcome. She goes half the distance
toward* BUS *before speaking. The* SALESMAN *watches
with curiosity*)

JACKIE Bus?
(BUS *turns to face her now. He has caught hold of
himself and has a big smile for her*)

BUS Jackie!

JACKIE How are you, Bus?

BUS Couldn't be better, Doll. Step right up here and
have a beer. Long time no see. How ya doin'?

JACKIE (*Joining him at the bar*) I'm all right, Bus.
(HOWIE *sets another beer before her*)

BUS By God, you're still the best lookin' doll I ever
saw.

JACKIE Thank you, Bus. You look wonderful. Really!

BUS It's the monkey suit. The girls always go for it.

JACKIE (*More serious now*) Bus . . . I just had to
see you. Why didn't you call me, Bus?

BUS Well . . . I din know whether a call from me'd
be very appreciated, Jackie.

JACKIE Oh, Bus, it would have been. Honest, Bus,
nothing that happened . . . was my fault. You know
how Daddy is. It . . . it just made me sick, what
happened.

BUS Drink your beer, Doll.

JACKIE I was praying you'd call me, Bus. I wanted so
to hear your voice . . . to see you again . . .

BUS I ran into trouble with your old man once, Jackie.
I din want to again.

JACKIE   There's no reason to be afraid of him any more. He's changed.

BUS   Yah?

JACKIE   You know . . . he drinks. He . . . he doesn't know much that goes on any more. I . . . I do anything I want to now.

BUS   Well, that's great. You got your car outside? How 'bout drivin' over to the next county and pickin' up a bottle? We could stop at the Riverview, maybe, if it's still runnin'.

JACKIE   It is. My car's outside. Dance with me, Bus.

BUS   Dance? Here?

JACKIE   (*Running to the juke box to drop a nickel to play her favorite tune*)   Yes. Please.

BUS   O.K. We'll dance.
(*The music starts, and he takes her in his arms. They dance slowly and softly to the love song, neither of them speaking for a while*)

SALESMAN   (*Softly to* HOWIE)   That the boy . . . all the trouble was about?

HOWIE   Yah. That's him.

SALESMAN   And Del had him sent to prison?

HOWIE   Oh, it was a great big fluke. The boy was eighteen when it happened. The girl was seventeen. So, according to law, the girl was a minor and the boy wasn't. They sent him to some reform school, but they let him go after about a year. He's no criminal, and they knew it. If you ask me, Del's the one they shoulda sent to prison.

SALESMAN Yah. Gimme another beer, Howie.

(HOWIE *gives him a glass of beer and then begins to wash and dry glasses. The* SALESMAN *is content to sit drinking his beer, just watching the two young people dance. Both* JACKIE *and* BUS *have been silent in each other's arms. Now* JACKIE, *as though rising out of a heavenly dream, speaks*)

JACKIE Oh, Bus, I've been telling myself all day that maybe I'd see you tonight, and maybe be dancing with you again, after all these years.

BUS Yah. It's great, Doll.

JACKIE Bus . . . I missed you terribly after you'd gone.

BUS Yah? Well . . . same here.

JACKIE I was so afraid you'd think it was my fault . . . what happened.

BUS No, Doll. I never blamed it on you.

JACKIE Oh, Bus, I missed you so, I was afraid I'd go crazy. Honest. I wanted to talk to you, just to talk to you, and be with you. Why didn't you answer my letters, Bus?

BUS Hell, Jackie. I didn't know what to say.

JACKIE I know.

BUS (*Trying to sound more cheerful*) Hey, I thought you'd be an old married woman by now.

JACKIE No.

BUS How come?

JACKIE Oh, I've dated a few boys since you left, but they didn't seem to mean anything.

BUS (*In a tone of inquiry*) Yah?

JACKIE (*Daring to ask it*)   How 'bout you, Bus? Have
. . . have you fallen in love with anyone?

BUS   No. Not me. I don't fall in love any more.
(*They have stopped dancing now and stand far away
from the bar, clinging to each other, talking in soft,
repressed voices*)

JACKIE   Bus, I'll always remember when we first started
going together.

BUS (*A memory he has not tried to recall*)   Oh . . .
yah.

JACKIE   Remember how shy we were of each other for
so long?

BUS   Yah. I remember.

JACKIE   You used to walk me home from school in the
afternoon, and we'd sit together on my doorstep for
hours, and not say a word.

BUS (*Obviously not giving himself to the recall*)   Sure,
sure.

JACKIE   And the first time you kissed me. Oh, I'll never
forget. Remember how scared we were when we made
love, feeling so guilty and afraid. You used to tell
me I was like some wonderful princess . . .

BUS   I'd forgotten I was so corny.

JACKIE   But we really felt those things, Bus. And when
you really feel them, they're *not* corny. And I used
to think of you as a god. I did. When we studied about
Greece in Ancient History, and read about their gods
and goddesses, I always visualized you, Bus, as Mer-
cury, and Mars, and Apollo.

BUS   Well . . . I guess you had me wrong, Doll.

JACKIE   Oh, Bus, I was in love with you. I've been in
love with you ever since, all these years. Every time
I went out with another boy, I was mad because he
wasn't you.

BUS   (*Turning it into a joke*) Hey, I guess I feel
flattered.

JACKIE   All these years I've been wanting to tell you.
I'm still in love with you, Bus. I guess I always will be.

BUS   Well . . . that's great. You know I think a lotta
you, too, Doll. I sure as hell do.

JACKIE   Did you ever know what happened to me, Bus?
Daddy took me to some doctor in Forth Worth, and I
had an abortion. Oh, Bus, it was terrible. I almost died.
I really wanted to die, Bus. I wanted the baby so bad.
(BUS *is not capable of dealing with this outpouring of
sorrows. He is at a loss for words*)

BUS   Jackie, I . . . I just don't know what to say.

JACKIE   And then I came back here and heard what had
happened to you. Oh Bus, I was despondent. I . . . I
tried to kill myself, Bus. I did. Then Daddy sent me to
a mental hospital in Kansas. I was there for about a
year. For a long time, they wouldn't even let me out of
my room without a guard.

BUS   (*Feeling more at a loss*) Yah . . . well, look,
Doll, it's not doing any good, goin' over all this . . .

JACKIE   I've wanted to tell you, Bus. I've wanted to tell
you for so long now.

BUS   O.K., now you've told me. I been through bad
times, too. Let's forget it. What d'ya say?

JACKIE   Kiss me, Bus. (*There is a hesitant pause*) It's
all right. I don't care if they see us. Kiss me.

BUS   Sure, Doll! (*Eagerly, he takes her in his arms and kisses her long and satisfyingly*) How was that, Doll?

JACKIE (*Clinging to him*)   Oh, Bus!

BUS   You still know how to cuddle, don't you, Doll?

JACKIE   Bus, don't make fun.

BUS   Who says I'm makin' fun? Look, Doll, you wait here a minute while I make a telephone call, will ya? (*She stays planted as* BUS *hurries to the telephone booth.* HOWIE *and the* SALESMAN *have other things to talk about now*)

SALESMAN   Ya know, it always depresses me, kinda, to come back to this town now. It's so run-down now, compared with what it used to be. It used to be such a pretty town, with all them fine homes on Maple Street, a fine car settin' in every driveway, the lawns all trim and green.

HOWIE   Yah. Things change.

SALESMAN   They sure as hell do. Mosta them homes now are boarding houses, aren't they?

HOWIE   The Baker home is a funeral parlor.

SALESMAN   Yah. One of the finest houses in town and now it's a funeral parlor. This hotel's run-down, too. They don't even have a porter. It used to be a fine place to stay, but now it's the crummiest hotel on my route.

HOWIE   Wouldn't doubt it.

SALESMAN   Gimme one more beer, Howie. Then I'm goin' to bed.

(HOWIE *draws another beer and sets it before him.* BUS *now comes hurrying from the telephone booth to report to* JACKIE)

BUS   Look, Doll, they got a cabin for us at the Riverview. Why don't we pile in your car, drive into the next county and pick up a bottle, and then stop at the Riverview and throw a ball. What d'ya say, Doll?

JACKIE (*Dumbly*)   The Riverview?

BUS   Sure, Doll! Look, I've been cooped up with the Old Man all week now, and I wanta let off a little steam. Let's get goin', Doll.

JACKIE (*Shattered with disillusionment, she sobs and runs to the door*)   No. I don't want to go to the Riverview with you, or anywhere else.

BUS   Well, for cryin' out loud! (*He goes to her patiently*) Look, Doll, what's got into you all of a sudden?

JACKIE   Bus, you used to love me. I know you did. But you can't even pretend to now. You've just been making up polite answers to everything I've said. I'm just any other girl to you now that you can . . . can let off steam with, and then forget.

BUS   O.K., Doll. I'm not gonna talk you into it.

JACKIE   Oh, Bus, can't you remember the way we used to feel?

BUS   Maybe I don't want to.

JACKIE (*Hurt*)   Oh, Bus!

BUS   Come off it, Jackie. Come off it.

JACKIE   Goodbye, Bus.
(*She hurries outside now, and* BUS *makes a slow return to the bar.* HOWIE *is watching him, getting out his private bottle to pour him another shot*)

HOWIE   Thought you might need this.

BUS You're a pal. What the hell am I gonna do with myself till morning?

HOWIE How about goin' home and goin' to bed?

BUS I couldn't get to sleep. I come back to this little town, and I remember too many things to sleep. I just keep wantin' to get away, to get away.

HOWIE There's the Mexican Quarter. Some of those places stay open all night.

BUS Yah. (*Picks up the shot of whiskey*) Gimme a beer to chase this down with, Howie.

HOWIE O.K.

BUS B'lieve me, when I clear outa this town tomorrow, it's for good.
(*He downs the whiskey and begins drinking his beer. By this time, the* SALESMAN *is asleep, his head lying in one arm, curved over the bar. He snores and* HOWIE *taps him on the shoulder. The* SALESMAN *stirs*)

SALESMAN Huh? What . . . ? Oh, have I been asleep? What d'ya know? Well, I hope I'll be able to do that when I get into bed. What do I owe you, Howie?

HOWIE One-ten.

SALESMAN (*Taking money from his pocket*) There ya are. (*Gets up from stool*) Ho hum! Gotta get up in the morning and see my customers. Wish business was better. I sure do.

HOWIE Good night, Harry.
(*The* SALESMAN *goes off, wandering through the arch-way leading into the hotel lobby*)

BUS I'll finish this up in a minute, Howie, and let you close.
(*He takes a long drink of beer*)

HOWIE No hurry, Bus. Take your time. I gotta stay open till midnight, anyway, whether there's customers or not.
(BUS *wanders over to the juke box and drops a nickel, then wanders back to the bar. A slow, mean blues begins to play, full of a rasping trumpet*)

BUS Did ya ever feel . . . like ya had to destroy something . . . in order to live?

HOWIE No . . . no. I can't say that I ever felt that way, exactly.

BUS I do. Maybe it's just a part of growin' up.
(*Now* JACKIE *wanders back into the Fiesta Room. There is a shyness, a hesitancy about her.* HOWIE *is the first to see her*)

HOWIE You leave something behind, Jackie?
(*Now* BUS *turns around immediately to see her*)

BUS Jackie!

JACKIE Bus . . .
(*He hurries to her side, in the doorway*)

BUS You makin' a return engagement?

JACKIE Bus . . . I'll go with you.

BUS You will?

JACKIE Sure. I'll go.

BUS Look, Jackie, maybe we better not.

JACKIE I want to, Bus. I do.

BUS How about all this love talk?

JACKIE I won't say those things any more. I promise.

BUS They just don't go any more, Jackie. They just don't go.

JACKIE (*With a little laugh of deprecation*) I know . . .

BUS Love, to me, is something they put you in jail for.

JACKIE A doctor at the hospital told me . . . I was too sentimental about things.

BUS I'm in this business now strictly for kicks, Doll.

JACKIE I'll be . . . just an ordinary girl . . . you happen to pick up . . . and we'll throw a ball.

BUS That's it, Doll. (*He grabs her to him hungrily and presses a sensual kiss against her lips. The music from the juke box makes a mocking accompaniment. Then he throws a bill on the counter for* HOWIE) So long, Dad!

(BUS *wraps* JACKIE *in his arms and they hurry out together.* HOWIE *watches them, drying glasses*)

Curtain

THE RAINY
AFTERNOON

The scene is the interior of an old barn in a small Midwestern town. Outside it is raining a slow, constant drizzle. Inside the barn, two little girls, dressed in stolen fragments of their mothers' clothing, play at having tea, making the barn an imaginary house, using nail kegs and tool chests and barrels for furniture. At left is a crude stairway leading up to a loft that is totally darkened. Of the two girls, WILMA *is the older and more aggressive. She is perhaps ten.* BILLIE MAE *is only seven or eight. She plays the game with some uncertainty, as though she were depending on* WILMA *for instruction. Both girls have their dolls beside them, treating the dolls like children.*

WILMA   You've got to spank your baby to make her behave.

BILLIE MAE   Mine's behaving.

WILMA   No she isn't. She's crying all the time. Spank her. I spank mine all the time. See?
(WILMA *demonstrates*)

BILLIE MAE   Mine isn't crying.

WILMA   She is, *too.* Spank her!

BILLIE MAE   Well, all right!
(*Timidly she spanks her doll*)

WILMA   . . . and scold her.

243

BILLIE MAE   You're a bad baby. You're a bad baby.

WILMA   (*Resuming her role*)   I guess you weren't invited to the big party at the country club yesterday. All the society people were there. I wore a beautiful new dress to it. Mrs. Sylvester Jones was there. She's a cow. She was dressed in horrible clothes. And her manners are terrible.

BILLIE MAE   Are they?

WILMA   Yes. Mrs. Sylvester Jones is a terrible woman. I don't know why anyone invites her any place. I didn't even speak to her.

BILLIE MAE   I wanta go home.

WILMA   (*Her own voice*)   You can't.

BILLIE MAE   Why not?

WILMA   Because we're having a tea party, silly. You can't just get up and walk out of a tea party.

BILLIE MAE   I'm not having any fun.

WILMA   You don't know how to *play*.
(VIC BATES, *a boy of* WILMA's *age, pulls up at the door on his bicycle*)

VIC   What're you crazy girls doin'?

WILMA   What business is it of yours?

VIC   I just asked. I don't care what you're doin'.

WILMA   Then go away. Our mothers don't allow us to play with boys.

BILLIE MAE   (*Affirming*)   No. You go away.

VIC   Am I hurtin' anyone, just sittin' here on my bike?

WILMA   I thought you crazy boys were goin' on a hike.

VIC   Don't you see it's raining?

WILMA (*Making a face*)   Yah, yah, yah!

VIC   What've you got on your mothers' clothes for?

WILMA   We can put on our mothers' clothes if we want to, can't we, crazy?

VIC   I don't know what fun you crazy girls get outa playin' with dolls.

WILMA   Girls have as much fun as boys do.

BILLIE MAE   Yes. Girls have just as much fun as boys do.

VIC (*Getting off his bike, coming into the barn*)   My father just got a new De Soto.

WILMA   *My* father got a Pontiac.

VIC   I like a De Soto better'n an old Pontiac.

WILMA   Pontiac's the best car there *is*. I wouldn't have an old De Soto.

BILLIE MAE (*Spanking her doll*)   Be good, you bad baby!

WILMA (*To* VIC)   Wanta play house?

VIC   How do ya play house?

WILMA   I'll be the mother. You be the father, and Billie Mae will be our baby girl.

VIC   What do we do?

WILMA   You just pretend to be grownups. It's fun. Come on and try.

VIC   It sounds stupid.

WILMA   Come on and play.

VIC   Nothin' else to do.

BILLIE MAE   My mother says I'm not supposed to play with boys.

WILMA   Your mother doesn't have to know, scaredy-cat!

BILLIE MAE   (*Looking at* VIC)   I don't like boys. Boys are rough.

WILMA   Oh, they are *not,* silly.

VIC (*Coming into the barn*)   O.K., I'll give it a try. What do you want me to do?

WILMA   We just act like grownups. I know everything grownups do. I've watched my mother and daddy. I know everything they do.

VIC   Like what?

WILMA   You pretend like you're coming home from the office. You're real tired and I've got to get dinner.

VIC   What fun'll that be?

WILMA   (*Impatient with him*)   It's just the way you play the game.

VIC   O.K. (*Goes out and comes in again as a tired husband. He has no real gift for make-believe, but he tries to be convincing. He stretches his arms and flops into a chair*)   Sure had a busy day at the office today.

WILMA   Did you, Hubby dear? I played bridge with the Van Uppingtons! And afterward we took a ride in their Rolls Royce.

VIC (*Himself*)   We supposed to be real rich?

WILMA   Sure.

VIC (*Back into his role*)   I made fifty million dollars this afternoon. On the stock market.

WILMA   That's wonderful, dear. Now maybe I can get some new clothes. I'm so sick of all my old things.

VIC   I think maybe I'll get another new car. I think I could use a racing car, maybe.

WILMA   Would you like a cocktail, dear?

VIC   Sure.

WILMA   Baby's been very bad today, Hubby dear. I'm afraid you'll have to spank her.

VIC   All right.

WILMA   She just refused to do everything I told her to do, so you'll have to spank her to keep her from growing up to be a very bad girl.

VIC   All right.
      (*He picks up* BILLIE MAE *and starts to put her over his knee*)

BILLIE MAE   (*Accusingly, to* WILMA)   I don't think this is fair.

WILMA   It's just *pretending,* Silly.

VIC   (*Spanking her lightly*)   You must be a good girl, Baby dear, and do everything your mother tells you.

WILMA   You must spank her hard, Hubby dear. She's been a *very* bad girl.
      (VIC *spanks her harder*)

BILLIE MAE   (*Jumping off* VIC's *lap*)   I'm not going to play any more if you keep on spanking me.

WILMA   I guess she's been punished enough, Hubby dear. We'll let Baby go back to bed now and go into the living room.

VIC   O.K.

BILLIE MAE   (*To herself*)   I don't see why I have to be the baby.

WILMA (*To* VIC)   Would you like a cocktail, dear?

VIC   Sure.

WILMA (*Herself, to* BILLIE MAE)   You be our maid now and bring us cocktails.

BILLIE MAE   I'm not going to play any more. You didn't tell me I'd have to be the maid.

WILMA   Just bring us a tray with something on it. Then you can go back to being Baby.

BILLIE MAE   I'm not having any fun at all. (*Sets a couple of dirty old glasses on a board and serves drinks*) Here are your cocktails.

WILMA   Thank you, Maid. (BILLIE MAE *returns to the chest and sits there resuming the role of Baby.* WILMA *continues to* VIC) I don't know what we're going to do with Maid, Hubby dear. She's just a terrible maid. She won't do anything I ask her.

VIC   Tell her we're going to fire her.

WILMA   But we can't fire her because help is so hard to get.

VIC   Why don't *you* do the work?

WILMA   Rich society women like me never do their own work. The Van Uppingtons have fifty maids, and butlers, too. And chauffeurs. And . . . all kinds of servants. Do you like your cocktail, dear?

VIC   It's all right.

WILMA   Are you ready for dinner, dear?

VIC   I guess so.

WILMA (*Calling*)   Maid! Maid! Hubby and I are ready for dinner now.

BILLIE MAE (*In her own voice*)   You want me to be Maid again?

WILMA   Well, of course.

BILLIE MAE (*In her role*)   Dinner is served.

WILMA   Say "Madam."

BILLIE MAE   Madam.

WILMA   That's better. (*To* VIC) Will you take me to dinner, Hubby dear?

VIC (*Getting up*)   O.K.

WILMA   We're having roast turkey and banana salad and angel-food cake à la mode.

VIC   Can't we have some sweet potatoes, too? I like sweet potatoes.

WILMA   All right, dear. We'll have sweet potatoes, too. (*They sit, one on either side of a barrel which serves as a table, and* BILLIE MAE *hands them imaginary dishes*)

VIC   That's awful good turkey.

WILMA   It was the finest one I could buy. And isn't the banana salad good, too?

VIC (*Pretending to eat*)   Sure. It's good, too.

WILMA (*To* BILLIE MAE)   You can bring us the angel-food cake à la mode now.

BILLIE MAE   O.K.

WILMA (*To* VIC)   I certainly hope you like the dessert, Hubby dear.

VIC (*Himself*)   My mother just calls my father by his real name.

WILMA   I like to play the game the way *I'm* playing it.

VIC It just sounds kind of crazy, callin' me "Hubby dear" all the time. No one does that.

WILMA They do, too. (*Back in her role*) Have you had enough dinner, Hubby dear?

VIC I guess so.

WILMA Shall we go into the living room and look at television?

VIC I wanta go play poker.

WILMA You can't leave me alone with Baby.

VIC Oh, all right.

WILMA I'll put Baby to bed now. Will you come and kiss her good night?

VIC Have I gotta kiss her?

WILMA Well, sure, crazy! Are you afraid to kiss her?

VIC No. I'm not afraid. It's just kinda crazy. That's all.

WILMA (*To* BILLIE MAE) Daddy and I have come to say good night, Baby dear!

BILLIE MAE Good night!

WILMA Say your prayers and sleep tight.

BILLIE MAE O.K.
(WILMA *kisses* BILLIE MAE *on the cheek, then turns to* VIC)

WILMA Now it's your turn.
(VIC *leans over and kisses* BILLIE MAE *on the cheek*)

VIC Good night, Baby.

BILLIE MAE Good night, Daddy.

WILMA Shut your eyes real tight and go to sleep.

BILLIE MAE O.K.

WILMA   *Real* tight.

BILLIE MAE   I've got 'em shut as tight as I can.

WILMA   I want Baby to grow up to be a very good girl, don't you, hubby dear?

VIC   Yah . . . sure.

WILMA   I don't think I want to look at television, after all.

VIC   I don't care.

WILMA   I've had such a busy day, I'm awfully tired. I think I'll go to bed.

VIC   O.K.

WILMA   Are you ready to go to bed, too, Hubby dear?

VIC   Me? Oh . . .

WILMA   You've had such a busy day at the office. I think you should go to bed now and be sure to get your rest.

VIC   Well . . . I . . .

WILMA   Come on, Hubby dear.

VIC (*He is not acting now*)   Well . . . what do we do?

WILMA   Our bedroom is in the hayloft. We'll go up there and leave Baby down here.
(*She is completely self-possessed*)

VIC (*Clearing his throat*)   Uh . . . I don't think I wanta go to bed now. You go on to bed, and I . . . I'll go out for a walk.

WILMA   You can't. It's raining outside.

VIC   Oh!

WILMA   You're *scared*.

VIC   Who says so?

WILMA   It sure looks like it.

VIC   Well, I'm not, if you should happen to want to know.

WILMA   Well, come on then. It's just a game.

VIC   You mean . . . up there in the loft?

WILMA   Sure.

VIC   (*Completely at sea*) Well . . . I'm not gonna play this game any more. This is a crazy game. I'm not playin'.
(*He starts for his bike*)

WILMA   I *told* you you're scared. (VIC *stops. He's not going to let himself be called scared*) Boys are worse scaredy-cats than girls.

VIC   Well . . . gee whiz!

WILMA   And it's perfectly all right. There couldn't be anything wrong about it, cause we're just playing a game, aren't we? And we're doing everything our mothers and fathers do. So what could be wrong about it?

VIC   Well . . . I don't know, but . . .

WILMA   Unless you're just a plain old scaredy-cat.

VIC   I told you, I'm not scared.

WILMA   Then prove it!

VIC   You're sure crazy.

WILMA   *Prove* it!

VIC   Well . . . (*With a nod at* BILLIE MAE, *lying on the chest with her eyes shut*) What about her?

WILMA (*Whispering*) She won't have to know anything.

VIC Well . . . gee!

WILMA Come on, scaredy-cat!
(*She starts up the stairs to the loft*)

VIC Gee!

WILMA If you don't follow me in two minutes, you're
the biggest scaredy-cat that ever lived. So there!
(*Continues up the stairs*)

VIC Shut up, will ya? I'm comin'.

WILMA (*Stops and turns around*) Then come along.

VIC (*Following her, against his better judgment*) I'm
comin'. I'm comin'.
(*He follows* WILMA *into the darkness of the loft, and
there is a silence of several minutes. Then* BILLIE MAE
sits up and looks about her)

BILLIE MAE What're you kids doin'? (*There is no
response and she feels lonely and rejected*) What's
everyone doin'? (*Still no response.* BILLIE MAE *stands
and walks around the barn, stopping at the foot of the
stairs looking up*) What're you crazy kids doin' up
there in the loft? (*No response*) I bet you're doin'
something bad. (*No response*) You kids are doin'
something bad. (*No response.* BILLIE MAE *begins to
sob*) I don't like you any more, Wilma Wadsworth.
I don't like you at all. (*Still no response*) I'm going
home now and tell my mother . . . (*No response*)
and I'll never come over to play with you again. (*Apparently* WILMA *is not concerned.* BILLIE MAE *moves
to the door, as though hoping someone will stop her*)
I'm going. (*No response*) I'm going. (*No response.
Now, the feeling of rejection is too strong for* BILLIE

MAE *to hold. She bursts into sudden tears while she runs out of the barn*) I'll never come back here to play with you again. I hate you, Wilma Wadsworth. I'll never be your playmate any more. I hate you. I hate you.

(*The stage is empty now. There are several moments of absolute and mysterious silence*)

Curtain

*
THE MALL
* *

This is a play that has come out of my own fantasies about characters I have noticed on summer strolls through Central Park, people who seem to live in the park during permissible weather, people who seem reduced to the pursuit of the most basic human needs. It was an attempt to write a play that made its dramatic point by a kind of combustion of forces rather than by a real narration. I had just wanted to contrast certain kinds of love and dramatize people in their pursuit of love. I found most interesting the older man's blind desperation in search for love in contrast with the young people's almost accidental discovery of love.

The scene is the mall of an amusement park in a seaside resort town. The promenade stretches across the stage, benches at the back, the sea presumably being the audience. The time is early fall, late September or early October, and the park is out of season. Summer is past and there is a feeling of rejection in the atmosphere. Behind the mall, in the distance, one can see the vast, deserted structure of the Playland. A Ferris wheel, a roller coaster, a parachute ride loom up in the background, great and useless structures waiting for their season to return. Closer behind the promenade are the banners heralding the freaks, likenesses of whom are pictured on the banners in fading primary colors, in almost grotesque caricature.

On one of the benches at the back of the promenade, facing the audience, sit two old CRONES, *wine-heads, sharing a bottle of cheap wine from which they take occasional refreshing swallows. During the warm weather, they make the mall their home, bringing their wine there, sometimes sleeping there if they can avoid detection by the police. It is hard to imagine they have another home, if they do, for they and their garments are as weathered as the benches and the scenery surrounding them, all of which they seem a living part. They sit here through most of the day, observing the life around them,*

257

*nudging each other and cackling together in mutual ap-
preciation of the ironies they look for. On another bench
sit two middle-aged* MATRONS *who have lingered for a
short rest before returning to their respective homes after
one of their daily walks, which they make together in
the mutual hope of reducing. They have just sat down
and are fanning themselves and getting their wind. The*
CRONES *watch, with hawk eyes, their every movement, as
though they sought in the faces and actions of humanity
reassuring proof of life's futility; for the* CRONES *have decided to let life pass them by, and they could never admit
to a feeling of loss.*

MATRON 1   Sort of a muggy day, isn't it?

MATRON 2   Yes. I don't like a muggy day, do you?

MATRON 1   No, I don't like muggy days at all. September's a sad month, don't you think? (*A pause*) Or do
you let yourself think about things like that?

MATRON 2 (*Musing*)   Now I don't know . . . if I've
ever given the matter much thought. Let's see. Is
September a sad month? Well, yes! Of course it is,
isn't it? I mean, it's sad if you happen to like the
summertime as much as Fred and I and the children
do. Because in September, you know that summer's
over and wintertime is ahead, and the weather will
be cold. Yes. . . . (*Looking around her*) It's very
sad.

MATRON 1   I think so. (*She's the type who is given to
sudden changes of topic*) Did you weigh yourself this
morning?

MATRON 2 (*Nodding*)   I've lost *two* pounds.

MATRON 1   I wish *I* would.

MATRON 2   Oh, I'll probably put them right back on when I sit down to dinner tonight. I'm afraid the only way to lose weight is to go on a *severe* diet. I don't think these walks are doing either one of us any good.

MATRON 1   Well, I don't know about *you,* but I feel a hundred percent better.

MATRON 2   Oh, I feel better, too. It's so good for the circulation, but I don't think we're losing an ounce, either one of us. As a matter of fact, I think the walks are only making our flesh more solid. The only way to lose weight, I'm convinced now, is to go on a severe diet. Very severe.

MATRON 1   (*Sadly*)   Oh, dear! (*Her spirits back*) Well, we've sat long enough, don't you think?

MATRON 2   Yes I do. (*Looks at watch*) Besides, it's time I was getting home and fixing something for dinner.
(*Up from their bench now, they start to make their way across stage, down the promenade. They notice the* CRONES, *drinking and cackling, and assume a somewhat superior attitude*)

MATRON 1   Goodness, the people one sees here after sunset.

MATRON 2   It really isn't safe. Do you think we might trot?

MATRON 1   What?

MATRON 2   Maybe we'd lose more weight if we trotted . . . part of the time. I remember when I was a Girl Scout, we used to go on hikes, and we'd trot for fifty steps, then walk for fifty. That way, you don't get tired.

MATRON 1   Shall we try?

MATRON 2   I'm game.
(*Standing side by side, they start off together, trotting, as though beginning a long relay race. The* CRONES *watch them off, cackling hilariously, as though they had just observed the prize absurdity of all time.*)

CRONE 1   Oh, God, Sister, wouldn't it kill ya?

CRONE 2 (*Who is given to mocking imitations*)   "I have to go home now and fix something for the children. Junior needs all his strength 'cause he's layin' the new maid, and little Geraldine is always hungry when she gets back from the opium den."

CRONE 1   Oh, God, Sister, ain't they a riot?

CRONE 2   Every day that passes, I thank the stars that whatever I be now, I ain't one of *them*.

CRONE 1   If they wanta lose weight, why don't they *quit* eatin', like we do, and live on the bottle? That'd take off a few pounds.

CRONE 2   And make 'em merrier company, too, wouldn't it, Sister?

CRONE 1   Sure, sure.
(*Now a young* SAILOR *comes on, a good-looking fellow in his late teens. Apparently he is expecting to meet someone, and his face looks concerned. He glances at his watch and then leans on the balustrade at the back, preparing himself to wait. The* CRONES *notice him and nudge each other*)

CRONE 2 (*Apropos of the* SAILOR)   Is it time for the lovers? Are the lovers comin' out?

CRONE 1   It's *always* time for the lovers, Sister. Love goes around the clock.

CRONE 2 Waitin' for his sweet patootie, ain't he?

CRONE 1 Sure, sure.

CRONE 2 Handsome lad, ain't he? Or is he your type?

CRONE 1 (*Slapping her thighs and laughing*) Any type's *my* type, Sister.
(*They laugh uproariously together*)

CRONE 2 Every once in a while, I get to feelin' kinda spry even now, and I think of puttin' a few feathers in my hair and jewels on my fingers and goin' off somewhere to dance. Oh, God, Sister, remember the days we used to dance.
(*She gets to her feet and swings around in a waltz with an imaginary partner*)

CRONE 1 You can still do it, Sister. Graceful as a swan.

CRONE 2 (*Returning to the bench, winded*) Now I *can't,* Sister. Can't dance no more. I'm winded and weak already. Gimme the bottle.
(*She takes a long, satisfying swallow*)

CRONE 1 Well, you useda could. That's the important thing. You useda could.

CRONE 2 (*Holding her heart painfully*) Oh, God, Sister, that liked to did me in. I just ain't what I used t'be. That's all.
(BARNEY *and* DELL *come on. Both are men of around forty.* BARNEY *is a large man,* DELL *rather small.* BARNEY *wears no hat or necktie, and his suit, of a light washable material, is clean but unpressed. His shoes are scuffed and the frayed collar of his shirt is open at the neck.* DELL *wears the working clothes of a laborer. He is a slight man with large sad eyes. They are talking as they come on together*)

BARNEY (*Angrily impatient*)   Don't talk to me no more about it, Dell. I'm tellin' you to shut up.

DELL   Barney, I'm only tryin' to persuade you to take the doctor's advice.

BARNEY   Doctors or no doctors, I'm stayin' here till I find Clara.

DELL   Maybe Clara won't show up, Barney. It's been a long time and . . .

BARNEY   She'll be here. I know Clara.

DELL (*Hopelessly*)   Oh, Barney. . . .
(When the two men sit together on a bench, CRONE 2 *is quick to run to them with an outstretched hand)*

CRONE 2   Help a poor widow woman, sirs. My house burned down last night and I got no money to take care of me and the kids.
(The men pay her no more attention than they do the breeze. She lingers for a moment. Something she detects in the men makes her suspicious and she runs back to CRONE 1)

CRONE 2   Oh, God, Sister, I didn't like the smell of them.

CRONE 1   What ya mean, Sister?

CRONE 2   I've smelled that smell before and I don't like it. It's that disinfectant they use in them loony bins. Before they let you out, they give you clothes that have soaked in it. Oh, God, Sister, it's a frightful smell to *me*.
(She is frightened)

CRONE 1 (*Passing the bottle*)   Console yourself, Sister. I ain't gonna let 'em take ya back.
*(*CRONE 2 *takes a long swallow of the wine)*

DELL   Barney, the only thing for you to do is go out on that farm. You'd like it there, Barney. Things'd be quiet there and you could relax. There wouldn't be nothin' t'upset ya.

BARNEY   There ain't nothin' gonna upset me. I don't need to relax. I'm all right, I tell ya.

DELL   Barney, you *think* you're all right, but you're really not. You're still sick, Barney. The doctors said you was to keep quiet for a long time and not try to do much. They say if you get out and start chasin' gals again and start gettin' mad and excited and worked up again, you'll end up in the zoo again, in the same ward.

BARNEY   I been a long time in that zoo, and now I gotta have me a woman.

DELL   Clara's no *good* fer you, Barney. You know she ain't.

BARNEY   Clara loved me once, Dell.

DELL   You don't understand women like Clara, Barney. They love *every*body once.

BARNEY   But Clara's gonna love me again.

DELL   How ya figure that?

BARNEY   'Cause I got love streamin' outa my heart like heat from a furnace. And I can't let it go to waste. Someone has got to share it.

DELL   You're just buildin' yourself up to a big letdown, Barney. Lemme take you out to that farm, where it'd be peaceful and quiet.

BARNEY   (*With sudden ferocity*) Mother Dell, I'm gonna call ya. You're worse'n a God damn woman with your advice and warnings and protections.

DELL   Now, Barney, take it easy. I'm not sayin' no more. It's just that I want you to be all right, Barney. *You* know that. It's just that I want ya to be all right.

BARNEY   (*Rising to full height*)   God damn ya, don't you know you can't make me all right, whatever's the matter with me? Don't you know that every man's gotta find his salvation somewhere inside hisself? And that regardless how sick I be, and how mixed up inside me, no amount of preachin', no amount of coaxin' and needlin' and cautionin' is gonna do any good unless I feel some change in *here*. (*He pounds his breast*) That's where it's gotta come from.

DELL   I know, Barney.

BARNEY   And in *here* (*Indicating his heart*) somethin' won't lemme rest, till I find Clara.

DELL   I'm sorry, Barney. I won't say no more.

BARNEY   All right, then. Let's sit peacefully and wait till she shows up.

DELL   All right, Barney. Anything you say.
   (*The two men sit, looking straight ahead, rather gloomily at the sea.* BARNEY *always wears an expression of trying to figure out some worrisome problem. Now a young* GIRL, *exceedingly pretty, comes on to meet the* SAILOR)

GIRL   Have I kept you waiting long?

SAILOR   Not very, but it's seemed long.

GIRL   I got here as fast as I could. I had to lie to the folks to get out of the house. I told them I was going over to Helen's.

SAILOR   Gee . . . it's funny, isn't it?

GIRL   How d'ya mean?

SAILOR I mean . . . when I came ashore this time, I didn't realize anything like this was gonna happen.

GIRL I know what you mean.

SAILOR 'Cause I never felt like this before . . . 'bout a girl. No fool!

GIRL I never did either . . . about a *boy*.

SAILOR Ernie and I left the boat together . . . he says have I got plans . . . I says no . . . so he tells me his girl Helen might be able to bring a friend . . . and I almost said, "Don't bother." Then I figured . . . why not? And I met you.

GIRL And I almost didn't go when Helen called and asked me. 'Cause I met Ernie once before and didn't much like him. I just didn't s'pose he could have a friend . . . as nice as you.

SAILOR Ernie's not a bad guy. Kinda loud but . . . (*On second thought*) Hey! You're the only girl ever told me I was nice.

GIRL But you are.

SAILOR No I ain't. Not really. It's just that. . . . Well, when I'm with you, I *feel* nice . . . so then I'm nice. The rest of the time I'm pretty ornery . . . I think.

GIRL No one's perfect.

SAILOR No.

GIRL Gee, I . . . I hate to go.

SAILOR So do I. (*A pause*) I got till midnight. Couldn't you stay with me till then?

GIRL I just *can't*. I been out late the last three nights, and the folks are beginning to suspect something.

SAILOR   What the heck! You can do what you want to, can't you?

GIRL   I . . . I lied to you. I'm not twenty. I'm . . . seventeen.

SAILOR   Y'are? (*And as she nods*) I'm nineteen. But I been on my own since I was a kid.

GIRL   I promised the folks I'd be right back. I don't want 'em to call Helen's and find out I'm not there.

SAILOR   Well . . . I guess this is it.

GIRL   I guess. Will you write?

SAILOR   I never *have* wrote letters . . . but I'll try.

GIRL   Just once in a while. Or just drop a post card that says *love*.

SAILOR   Okay.

GIRL   And . . . I'll remember you . . . as long as I live. I know.

SAILOR   (*With a feeling of futility*) It just ain't fair. You go along your usual way, feelin' you're happy, takin' what comes, not carin' about too much one way or the other. . . . Then *zowie!* one day it happens. You fall in love. And it makes your whole life up until then seem kinda pointless. . . .

GIRL   That's the way *I* feel, too.

SAILOR   And then you can't just go back to your old life. 'Cause it don't seem no good.

GIRL   No. It don't.

SAILOR   (*Longingly*)   Can't you stay till my boat leaves?

GIRL   (*Frightened*)   I'll get an awful beating if I'm not back soon. My dad gets furious when I'm out late. I . . . I *gotta* go now.
(*The* SAILOR *takes her in his arms and kisses her*)

SAILOR   Goodbye!

GIRL   If you want me to, I'll not make any more dates till you come back.

SAILOR   I don't know . . . when I'll come back.

GIRL   (*Sobbing*)   I just can't bear to think I may never see you again.

SAILOR   Well . . . I'll probably be back in a year or so.

GIRL   A year!
(*The* GIRL *runs off now, crying. The* SAILOR *stands a few moments looking after her, then walks off sadly, in the other direction. The* CRONES *have watched the entire scene. They cackle quietly*)

DELL   (*To the* CRONES)   Can't you girls do anything but laugh?

CRONE 1   Might as well laugh as to cry, Mister.

CRONE 2   'Cause if you ever get started crying, you'll never stop.

DELL   It don't sound very respectful.
(CRONE 1 *sees a familiar figure in the distance*)

CRONE 1   (*Gloatingly*)   Here she comes, Miss La-De-Da!

CRONE 2   Dressed up in her Sunday best, out to find herself a *lovin'* man.

CRONE 1   She don't miss a night. That one! She can't go to sleep without her lovin' man.
(*They both cackle gluttonously.* CLARA [*Miss La-De-Da*] *comes strutting on, wearing a bright pink dress and shoes with high platform soles.* BARNEY *stands respectfully on seeing her approach*)

DELL   Let *her* come to *you,* Barney. Take my advice. (BARNEY *remains silent and nervously alert.* CLARA'S *first preoccupation is with the* CRONES)

CLARA   Why don't you old hags go off somewhere and die? (*The* CRONES *are invulnerable to any insult. They cackle*) Why don't you old witches get on your brooms and ride off into the sky? (*The* CRONES *cackle louder*) Old hags! Too old to have any fun yourselves. All you can do is sit here makin' fun of others. There oughta be a law against it. (*The* CRONES *continue to cackle*) *I'll* never be like you. I'm still young. And I still got what it takes to make 'em take a second look. And I'm gonna have my fun. See?
(*The* CRONES *cackle louder than ever. Angrily,* CLARA *comes center.* BARNEY *now must speak out.*)

BARNEY   Clara!

CLARA   My God! Where'd *you* come from?

BARNEY   They let me go, Clara. First thing I do is come to see you.

CLARA   *When* did they let you go?

BARNEY   Just this morning.

CLARA   You sure you didn't sneak out or break out?

BARNEY   Cross my heart, Clara, and hope to die.

DELL   He's on the level, Clara. The doctors told 'im he's okay. He still has to take it easy for a while, but he's okay.

CLARA   What're you doin' here?

BARNEY   This is where we met, Clara. Remember? I come back to get you.

CLARA   I told you a hundred times, it's all over 'tween you and I.

BARNEY (*With an almost childlike expression of hurt*)
You don't mean that, Clara.

DELL   Sure she does, Barney. C'mon, let's beat it.
What d'ya say? (*Trying to divert him*) *I* tell ya what,
I know a place where there's hunnerds of good-lookin'
women. Sure I do. Not so very far from here, either.
What ya say we go?

BARNEY (*Shoving* DELL *aside*)   Go way. (*Going to*
CLARA) I come back to get *you,* Clara. I'm taking
you with me.

CLARA   Says *you!*

BARNEY   I'm a new man, Clara. I got real love in my
heart. I wanta share it.

CLARA   Listen to that talk!

BARNEY   I mean it, Clara. You gotta gimme a chance.

CLARA   You *had* your chance. It's all over now. Can't
you get that through your thick skull? Now beat it.

BARNEY   I got real love in my heart, Clara. You don't
know what it is. But it's a wonderful thing, *real* love.
I know that now. There's nothin' in the world like it.

CLARA   Crap!

BARNEY   Real love, not just for a night or two, but for
always, when two people live as *one.* Think of it,
Clara. My life'd be yours. Your life'd be mine. Then
we'd both have a bigger life, Clara, a life that'd mean
somethin'.

CLARA   I never heard such crazy talk.

BARNEY   I know what real love *is,* Clara. I had it once,
long time 'fore I met you. I had it. It was wonderful,
Clara. My life was hers and her life was mine, and
we had real happiness together.

CLARA (*Exasperated*)   Oh, Lord! The same old line.

BARNEY   I gotta get that happiness back, Clara. Don't you understand?

CLARA   And can't *you* understand that I got enough happiness to suit *me*?

BARNEY   But you don't understand. I tell you what it's like. It's like you'd spent all your life livin' in one room, with the door closed, not knowin' that the door opened into another room, bigger, that looked out onto a beautiful view of the entire world. That's what *real* love is like, Clara.

CLARA (*To* DELL)   Why don't ya take him back to the zoo?

DELL   C'mon, Barney old boy. You oughta know when you're not wanted.

BARNEY (*Jerking himself free of* DELL)   God damn it, lemme be!

DELL   Take it easy, Barney.

BARNEY   I *been* in that other room, Clara. I know what real love is. I'd learn you.

CLARA   Now listen t'me. I come out here this evenin' 'cause I was expectin' to meet a very attractive gentleman that happened to speak to me th' other day as we was gettin' off the subway. He's due to show up any minute. Then we're goin' over to the Palace Ballroom and dance. I'd appreciate it if you was not around when he shows up.

BARNEY   Clara!

DELL   You heard what she said, Barney. C'mon!

BARNEY (*Angrily insistent now, seizing* CLARA *in his arms*)   God damn it, you're goin' *with* me. I got real

love in my heart and I'm gonna learn ya what it is.
You'll be happy after you know. We'll both be happy,
Clara. Happier'n you ever thought you could be.

DELL (*Turning his face, fearful of watching the scene*)
Barney . . . you mustn't do things like that.

CLARA (*A tigress now, she kicks* BARNEY *in the groin
and slaps at him viciously*)   Lay your hands off me,
you maniac bum, or I'll call a cop and he'll take you
back to the zoo where ya belong. I've heard enough
of your love talk, and I ain't gonna listen to any more.
I'm free, white and over twenty-one, and I don't have
to put up with any more of this crap if I don't wanta.
And I don't *wanta*. Can't you get that through your
lunatic skull?

BARNEY (*Fallen to the ground, cringing like a big, hearty
dog that is punished for being too affectionate*)
Clara! Clara!

DELL   Clara, you shouldn't a done that. Barney's been
sick.

CLARA   He's makin' *me* sick now.

BARNEY (*Doubled up in pain*)   Clara, you was sweet to
me once.

DELL   Fight back, Barney. Even if she *is* a woman.
Fight back.

BARNEY   I can't, Dell.

DELL   You always was a great fighter. Makes me sick
to see you like this.

BARNEY   I can't fight . . . A man in *love*, Dell, has
got no fight.
    (BARNEY *remains squatting on the ground*, DELL
    hovering over him protectively. The CRONES *cackle*

with an appreciation of irony. The SAILOR *and the* GIRL *now come on from opposite sides of the stage, walking very slowly, tentatively toward each other. There is an occasional sob and whimper from* BARNEY. CLARA *walks restlessly about the mall, looking occasionally into the distance for her date)*

SAILOR (*Walking very slowly toward the* GIRL)   I . . . I just can't seem to go.

GIRL (*Coming slowly toward the* SAILOR)   I can't either.
(*They meet now, center stage, and grasp each other passionately, then melt in a sustained kiss*)

CRONE 1 (*Transfixed by the scene of the* SAILOR *and his* GIRL)   Oh, God, Sister, remember the days we had love?

CRONE 2 (*With a wistful countenance of momentary pain*)   Yes, Sister . . . I remember.

CLARA (*Apparently sees her friend in the distance*)   It's about time.
(*She waits at stage right. It is dusk now and the sky is beginning to darken*)

SAILOR (*With the* GIRL *in his arms*)   Maybe we could do something crazy . . . like gettin' married.

GIRL   Anything you say.

SAILOR   Just stay with me . . . as long as you can.

GIRL   I will.

SAILOR   What'll you do about your old man?

GIRL   I don't know.

SAILOR   Will he beat you?

GIRL   Prob'ly.

SAILOR   Cri-miney!

GIRL   It's all right. I don't care.
(*They sit together in a fast embrace. The two* CRONES *gaze on them as though they were figures in a dream*)

CRONE 1   You're cryin', Sister.

CRONE 2   Am I?

CRONE 1   I am, too. We gotta stop.

(BARNEY *still remains on the ground, nursing his wounds.* DELL *still is with him. Now* CLARA'S *boy friend comes on, a* MAN *close to forty, good-looking, sharply dressed.* CLARA *becomes very seductive, a sly insinuation in her voice*)

CLARA   Well . . . good evening!

MAN   Same to you.

CLARA   Are you the man who said you'd take me to the Palace Ballroom?

MAN   I'm the man.

CLARA   Well . . . I'm waitin'.

MAN   . . . Unless . . . you had some other place in mind, perhaps. Some place . . . more private.

CLARA   I do . . . but we'll have time for that later.

MAN   'Cause when I look at *you,* Baby, I got other things on my mind than dancin'.

CLARA   (*Laughing coarsely*)   How many girls you said that to?

MAN   Hell, I don't know. But every time I say it, I *mean* it, Baby.

CLARA   C'mon, Daddy. Let's paint that ballroom red.
(*They strut off together arm in arm, the* CRONES, *of*

course, watching and cackling. It is night now. BARNEY *staggers to his feet to watch them after they have disappeared. Then he calls out in a shattering voice.*)

BARNEY Whore! Bitch! That's all y'are ,a two-bit whore! A two-timin' bitch!

DELL Take it easy, Barney. There's cops around.

BARNEY (*Falling to the ground, pounding it with his fists, sobbing hysterically*) Oh, God! And sweet, sweet Jesus! Where is there someone who can take my love? Where is there someone who can bear it?

DELL (*Sympathetically*) I told ya that's what'd happen, Barney.
(BARNEY *bawls like a wounded stag, as* DELL *kneels by his side attentively. The two* CRONES *cackle from their perch in the background. The* SAILOR *and his* GIRL *sit on a bench in a fast embrace. The two* MATRONS *return, trotting together. They stop for a moment to get their wind, and take notice of the characters around them*)

MATRON (*Apprehensive*) Oh, goodness! Let's not stay here.

MATRON 2 No. This is no place for us.
(*They trot off together*)

Curtain

*

AN INCIDENT AT
THE STANDISH ARMS

* *

*The scene is the rather pretentiously stylish living room
of a luxurious apartment in a large American city. When
the curtain rises the stage is empty. Suddenly, a* WOMAN
*comes running into the room as though fleeing someone.
She is quite an attractive woman in her mid-thirties,
dressed now in a filmy negligee, her bare feet in satin
sandals, her long, wavy hair loose. There is a desperation
about her now, as though she hoped to find a secret panel
somewhere in the walls that would suddenly open and
provide a means for her disappearance. But she can only
clutch at the air blindly and stifle the compulsory screams
in her throat. There being no magic exit, she finally runs
to a corner of the room like a guilty child seeking her
own punishment. She stands there waiting breathlessly
for the* MAN *to appear. After a few moments, he appears,
coming from the same room from which the* WOMAN
*came, presumably a bedroom. He is a big dark man of
rough good looks, maybe an Italian. He is a taxicab
driver, and he looks now for the cap which he left in the
living room before entering the bedroom. When he comes
out, he is buttoning his shirt. He looks at the* WOMAN
amused and mystified.

MAN Lady, fer Chris' sakes, whatsa matter? (*The*
WOMAN *trembles in her corner but she cannot answer*)
I ask ya, whatsa matter, lady? Ya got sick?

277

WOMAN (*Refusing to look at him, gasping her words*)
Go! Please go!

MAN Oh, so that's it. Ya wanta get rid a me now, don't
ya? Is that it?

WOMAN Please . . . I don't wish to seem rude . . .
but I . . . I really must ask you to go now.

MAN Whatsa matter? Don't I look so good to ya now
that it's all over?

WOMAN Please try to understand. I don't wish to seem
rude. I wouldn't be rude to you for anything in the
world. But I . . . I must be alone now.

MAN Whatsa matter? Is Papa on his way home? That
it? You're scared Papa's gonna come home and find
me here?

WOMAN (*Imploringly*)   Please! Please!

MAN Look, lady, what's so terrible if someone does
find me here? I brought you home in a cab, din I?
Maybe I helped you carry your packages up here to
your apartment.

WOMAN I . . . I have a young daughter. She'll be
coming home from school any minute now.

MAN What do you think I'm gonna do, stay here and
make faces at her?

WOMAN The . . . the management of the Standish
Arms . . . They're very observing . . . I . . . I
would be terribly embarrassed if they . . . if they
suspected anything.

MAN Look, lady, I got a family, too. I got three kids.
Yah. I don't want trouble no worse'n you do. You
ever stop to think a that?

WOMAN I . . . I haven't a husband any more . . . I . . . I'm divorced.

MAN Sure. I figured that. Look, lady, you could spare me just one little drink before I go, couldn't ya?

WOMAN (*Pointing*) There's the bar. You can help yourself. I . . . I'll have one, too.
(*The* MAN *pours two drinks. She downs hers in one gulp. He is more relaxed*)

MAN Jesus, I never saw such a change in anyone. You got in my cab down town, and I thought "Gee, here's a real doll. I could go for a littla that." Then, I could see ya lookin' at me from the back seat. Yah, I could see you were kinda goin' for me, too.

WOMAN I . . . I only thought you looked like someone I . . . once knew.

MAN Anyway, you liked what you was lookin' at, baby. Don't deny it.

WOMAN I . . . I don't deny it. I . . . I did notice you.

MAN Look, baby, this happens to me a lot. Yah. Sometimes I get a broad that wants to pay for her ride that way. I say, nothin' doin'. You'd be surprised, lady, some a the homes I been invited into, in this town. Plenty a places, just as knocked out as the Standish Arms.

WOMAN I . . . I'm really not interested.

MAN But I never saw a dame *turn* like you do. You ask me to come up to your apartment, and you throw yours arms around me when we get here and start givin' me the works . . .

WOMAN (*Hiding her face*) Please!

MAN And then it's all over and ya can't wait for me to get out. Ya can't even look me in the face. What kind of a dame are you?

WOMAN I . . . I really shouldn't have . . . asked you up. It was wrong of me. I . . . I don't know what made me do it.

MAN Well, *I* know what made you do it, lady, and if you don't, you better get wise to yourself. You're a sexy broad.

WOMAN Please! Don't say that.

MAN Most girls'd think I was givin' 'em a compliment.

WOMAN It's just that I get very lonely at times, since I was divorced, and I . . . I miss my husband in these ways, and . . .

MAN Lady, I understand. You don't have to tell me a thing. I'm only too glad to oblige.

WOMAN No. It isn't right. It isn't right.

MAN Well . . . I don't argue with myself about things like that.

WOMAN Please! When you go down, would you take the service elevator? And go out the back way? If the elevator man and the doorman see you, they'll become suspicious.

MAN Oh, fer Christ sake!

WOMAN I hate to ask it of you, but surely you understand.

MAN Yah. I understand. (*There is a pause*) Look, lady. This whole thing was your idea to begin with, and I'm not makin' any complaint even now, but . . . I hate to leave a woman like this, feelin' like I'd done dirty

on her somehow. Couldn't ya give me a li'l house
now? How 'bout it, huh? (*He places an appealing
hand on her shoulder*) C'mon, let's have a li'l kiss
before I go, shall we? Just to show we can be friends.
I ain't gonna pester ya, fer Christ sake. I'll probably
never see you again. But . . . let's leave off friendly.
How's about it?

WOMAN (*Shrinking*)   Not now. I . . . I couldn't.

MAN (*Now anger and insult seize him*)   Then God
damn you and your hypocrite ways! To hell with you
and all your kind. (*He seizes a costly Chinese vase
from a table and flings it to the floor*) You've made me
feel cheap, God damn you! You've made me feel
cheap!
(*He jerks his cap onto his head and bolts out of the
door, slamming it behind him. The* WOMAN *shrieks
and falls to the floor*)

WOMAN   My God, what have you done? What did you
do that for? How can I ever explain? (*With hurried
anxiety, she picks up the pieces of the vase and dumps
them into a wastebasket. Then she falls onto the divan,
shaking with tears and humiliation, crying out in a sort
of frantic prayer*) Oh, God, what makes me do these
things? Dear God, what makes me do them?
(*She lies prostrate on the divan, shaking and sobbing.
In several minutes, her young daughter, aged twelve,
enters, and the* WOMAN *sits up, drying her eyes, assuming her normal respectable posture*)

GIRL   I'm home, Mama. I'm home.

WOMAN (*Embracing the girl*)   Hello, dear!

GIRL (*In an indignant voice*)   Mother, I want you to
write a note to my teacher and ask her please to change

my seat, because there's a perfectly horrid girl who sits across from me. She uses all sorts of filthy words, and she stinks because she never bathes, and she wears ugly, dirty dresses. I refuse to go to school if I have to sit next to anyone like her. Promise me you'll write the note to my teacher, Mother. Promise me.

WOMAN   Yes, dear. I promise.

Curtain

THE STRAINS
OF TRIUMPH

Success is counted sweetest
By those who ne'er succeed.
To comprehend a nectar
Require sorest need.

Not one of all the purple host
Who took the flag today
Can tell the definition,
So clear, of victory,

As he, defeated, dying,
On whose forbidden ear
The distant strains of triumph
Break, agonized and clear.

EMILY DICKINSON

The scene is laid at the side of a small hillock behind which lies an open field. In the far background are bright-colored pennants flying in the breeze, and we hear the distant sound of strident band music, proclaiming victory. Mixed with the music is the sound of cheering voices.

VOICES Give 'em the axe, the axe, the axe!
Give 'em the axe, the axe, the axe!
Yeh for Simpson!
Simpson won the fifty-yard dash!
Next event!
Ready for the next event!
Give 'em the axe, the axe, the axe!
Give 'em the axe, the axe, the axe!
(*An* OLD MAN, *bent over his cane, comes walking onto the scene, drawn by the music and voices. He goes to the top of the hillock and stands, his back to the audience, watching the games in the distance. Now a young girl,* ANN, *comes running, laughing onto the scene. She is about nineteen, pretty, dressed simply in sweater and skirt, her hair free. Following fast behind her is* TOM, *a young athlete, dressed in the gray sweat suit and track shoes provided by his college. He catches up with* ANN, *grabs her in his arms and kisses her. Then they laugh lovingly together.* ANN *suddenly notices the*

285

OLD MAN, *who thus far has not turned to watch the young people but still stands, his back to the audience, looking off into the distance*)

ANN   He'll see.

TOM   What if he does? (*Thoughtless but not cruel*) He's just an old man.

ANN   Still, he can see us.

TOM   What if he does see us? What if he does? (*He grabs her in his arms and kisses her again. Then he proclaims loudly, attracting the* OLD MAN'S *attention*) Look, everybody! I'm kissing Ann. Ann and I are in love. I'm kissing her. See? (ANN *in his arms, he looks closely into her eyes*) Now, I've told the whole world, and the whole world may be watching. Does that keep me from kissing you?

ANN   Tom, Ben will be coming along any minute, and I don't want Ben to know.

TOM   (*Recklessly*)   To hell with Ben!

ANN   But I *like* Ben.

TOM   You *like* Ben, but you're in *love* with me. Admit it.

ANN   I do admit it, Tom.

TOM   Then forget about Ben. That's the only thing you can do. Forget him.

ANN   I don't want to hurt his feelings.

TOM   But you've *got* to hurt his feelings.

ANN   I mustn't. Ben and I grew up together. I know how deeply he feels things, much more than he shows.

TOM   I've had *my* feelings hurt, fer crying out loud! Before I came to college, I was nuts about a girl in high school, and she gave me the air. Yah! For a long time after that, I couldn't eat, I couldn't study, I didn't wanta see anyone. But I got over it. I learned to take it. It's just part of growing up.

ANN I know. The same thing happened to me in high school. I was awfully fond of a boy and he started dating my best friend. I cried and cried and cried. I sulked around the house until Mother took me to see a doctor. Do you know what he did? He gave me vitamin shots. Honestly!
(*They laugh*)

TOM But you got over it, didn't you?

ANN (*Their mood is still jovial. Their present love is too much with them for the past to cast a gloom*)   Yes, I got over it.

TOM And that's what Ben has got to do. Get over it. Even if he *is* my buddy, I gotta admit, he's spoiled. He's gotta learn to take his medicine like everyone else.

ANN (*Troubledly*)   I think he's suspected something already.

TOM After the races, we'll tell him.

ANN Both of us?

TOM Why not? We'll go to him together and say, "Ben, Ann and I are in love. She's going to wear my fraternity pin. Sorry, old man. These things are tough, but human beings always get over 'em. It's just part of growing up."

ANN I dread telling him. But I'll feel better about it if we're together.

TOM Just think, Ann. We'll always be together *now*.
(*He takes her in his arms*)

ANN (*Truly in love*) Oh, Tom!
(*He kisses her*)

TOM We're as one person already. Aren't we?

ANN Yes, Tom. I feel it, too.

TOM It's a magical process, *love,* isn't it? One day, two
people are separate individuals, each going his own
way; on another day, they meet and fall in love, and
they become like one. Without you now, I'd feel just
half a man.

ANN I feel the same, but I never realized, before we
met, that I was incomplete in any way.

TOM (*Taking her in his arms again*) Oh, Ann!

ANN Tom!
(*He kisses her again, while the* VOICES *and music
come up from the background. The* OLD MAN *watches,
his back still to the audience. He jumps up and down
with enthusiasm*)

VOICES Yea! Yea! (*In a chant*) V-I-C-T-O-R-Y!
That's the way to spell it!
Here's the way to yell it! (*A bombastic shout*)
VICTORY!
Yeh! Yeh! Pin a medal on Cutler! Cutler won the
hurdles. Yeh! Yeh!

TOM (*Releasing* ANN) Did you hear that? Cutler won
the hurdles. This is a big day for us. We better go back.

ANN Can't we sit together until your event?

TOM *Some*how. We'll manage somehow.
(*They run off together arm in arm. Slowly* BEN *comes
on from behind the hillock, where he stands for a few*

moments, watching ANN *and* TOM *disappear. One must get the feeling that he has been watching them and knows in his heart what has happened. First there is a look of intense anguish on his face, and he stands rigid with bitterness and rage. Then gradually the intensity subsides, and his features and his body relax into sad resignation, and he lopes down the hillock, getting to the bottom, letting himself fall to the ground, lying sprawled there. Slowly, the* OLD MAN *takes cognizance of him and, still standing at the top of the hillock, speaks)*

OLD MAN (*In the gentlest voice*)   Have you been hurt?

BEN (*Lifting his head*)   I'm all right.

OLD MAN   Is there anything the matter?

BEN (*A pause elapses while he considers the question and decides to avoid answering. Instead he asks directly*)   Who are you?

OLD MAN   I recently heard myself referred to as "just an old man." That's true, of course, but my students refer to me as Professor Benoit, Associate in the Department of Ancient Languages.

BEN   I apologize for not recognizing you, Professor.

OLD MAN   No one ever recognizes a professor. Don't apologize. (*There is a long pause.* BEN *is trying to hold back tears. The* OLD MAN, *perhaps sensing* BEN'S *despair, tries to sound diverting*) There's such a crowd there, isn't there? I honestly believe I never saw so many people. Wouldn't the Board of Regents be pleased if my classes started filling up that way? (*Suddenly* BEN *bursts out in uncontrollable tears. The* OLD MAN *is very concerned, hurrying down to* BEN'S *side*) My boy! My boy!

BEN (*Fighting off the* OLD MAN'S *almost motherly protec-tion*)   Go away, old man. Go away!

OLD MAN (*He seems to understand and withdraws, going back to the top of the knoll*)   Very well. I'm sorry I interfered. I shall mind my business and continue watching the games.
(*Now he stands as he did before, his back to* BEN, *who lies face down on the ground, all but writhing with the pain of his rejection. Background* VOICES *and music come up again. The band, with "Boola Boola," and the cheering squad start off in unison, the voices sounding vindictive*)

VOICES   Give 'em the axe, the axe, the axe!
Give 'em the axe, the axe, the axe!
Give 'em the axe!
Give 'em the axe!
Give 'em the axe! Where?
Right in the neck, the neck, the neck!
Right in the neck, the neck, the neck!
Right in the neck!
Right in the neck!
Right in the neck there!
(*Now the* VOICES *seem to explode into a vocal shower of calls, whistles and shrieks*)

OLD MAN (*His back to the audience, speaking to himself and anyone who cares to listen*)   I look forward to the games all year long. Last October I bought my season ticket to the Student Activity Program and have attended all the events during the year. I hap-pened upon this little knoll a few years ago when I was out on one of my walks, and I saw what a splendid view it offers of the stadium, so I've been coming here, where I enjoy being a solitary spectator.

You see, I'm rather a childish old man, and I get so
excited watching the games that I'm embarrassed for
others to see me, particularly my students, who surely
would think I had taken leave of my senses if they
saw me jumping up and down and pounding the air
with my fists. (*He gives a little chuckle*) So I gave
my ticket to the cleaning woman. And it pleased me
to do that, for I can't afford to pay her much and she
loves the games, too. *Every*one loves the games.
Although not everyone cares to contend in them. I
never did care to. I was studious even as a child. And
I was frail. I was always getting a nosebleed. So I
made myself content to watch and not participate. I
suppose all people are divided into two groups, those
who participate and those who watch and observe.
Sometimes, in my more melancholy moments, I wonder
if I have lived life at all, if my life has not been, rather,
a period of observation on earth, watching others live,
studying the way they live and commenting on their
success or failure in the process. Being very moved by
them at times, but still detached so that my envy of
their success is fleeting, and my sadness at their failure
passes when I sit down at a good meal or take a glass
of sherry. *Once* I was in love, and it terrified me. She
was so beautiful, so tender, so fine that I trembled in
her mere proximity. The reality of her seemed too
much for me to bear, and I fled. I could not accept
the responsibility of loving her. (*He sighs*) Alas! sometimes I am very lonely, of course. I go to bed, some
nights, despondent, but I always awake feeling free.
But I must admit, I always hurry to my office to
become involved in my research as quickly as possible,
for if I remain idle very long, I sometimes become
very depressed.

(*A rousing cheer comes from the stadium*)

VOICES   V-I-C-T-O-R-Y!
That's the way to spell it.
Here's the way to yell it!
VICTORY!
Yeh! Yeh!
Hopkins won the discus!
Yeh, Hopkins!
He's our boy! Yeh, Hopkins!

OLD MAN   They're putting Ronnie Hopkins up on their
shoulders now, carrying him through the stadium. I
had the lad in class last year. I found him at times
almost belligerent about learning, or about not learning. "What do I care about ancient history?" he
used to bellow. "Why should I spend my time worrying about what happened in the past? *I'm* living *now*."
"True," I always replied to him, "but sometimes the
present means more to us if we see it in terms of what
has been before." He would shake his head then and
mumble some incoherent protest. After grave consideration, I finally passed him in the course but with
a very low grade. He never even learned to spell
Nebuchadnezzar.

VOICES   Yeh, Hopkins!
He's our boy!
Trot him round the field again!

OLD MAN   (*Turns his back on the scene in the stadium and
looks down at* BEN, *who still lies sprawled at the foot
of the hillock, his face in his hands*)   Where do you
come from, young man?

BEN   (*Lifting his face, wiping away a few tears with the
back of his hand*)   A little town . . . in Iowa.

OLD MAN   I was through Iowa once on a train.

BEN   I wish to God I was back there.

OLD MAN   It never does any good to go back. Our memory always idealizes the past. If we return to it, we never find there what we're seeking.

BEN   Maybe.

OLD MAN   What are you studying here at the University?

BEN   I . . . I hope to become an architect.

OLD MAN   And you're an athlete, too? Remarkable.

BEN   I'm supposed to run in the relays.

OLD MAN   But aren't you going to?

BEN   I . . . I don't think so.

OLD MAN   But they'll be waiting for you at the stadium.

BEN   Let them.

OLD MAN   They're counting on you.

BEN   What if they are!

OLD MAN   I should think you'd be eager to start your race.

BEN   I was . . . until a few minutes ago.

OLD MAN   And now?

BEN   (*Slowly, with bitter distaste*)   Races suddenly seem . . . hateful and terrifying.

OLD MAN   Why?

BEN   I never knew before . . . what it is to lose.
      (*Another shout of victory goes up*)

VOICES   Yeh, Pomeroy!
      Give 'em the axe, the axe, the axe!
      Give 'em the axe, the axe, the axe!
      Yeh! Yeh!

OLD MAN (*Still in thought, responding to* BEN)   Yes, it's terrifying—to lose.
(*Two young* ATHLETES, BEN'S *age, run on together*)

1ST ATHLETE   Hey, Ben, we been lookin' all over for you.

2ND ATHLETE   You're in the next event. Get goin'.

OLD MAN (*Gently urging him*)   Go on, young man.

BEN (*To the other* ATHLETES)   Why should I?

1ST ATHLETE   What?

2ND ATHLETE   For crying out loud, Ben, you can't let us down.

BEN   I'm not going to run in the race.

1ST ATHLETE   Well . . . I'll be a . . .

2ND ATHLETE   Have you gone nuts?

OLD MAN   Young man, think carefully about this. Try to persuade yourself . . .

BEN   I've made up my mind.
(*There is a long pause*)

1ST ATHLETE   What'll we tell the coach, Ben?

BEN   Whatever you like.

2ND ATHLETE   Who'll he put in your place?

BEN   He'll find someone.

1ST ATHLETE (*Angrily*)   You're a lousy sport.

2ND ATHLETE   I agree.

BEN   I suppose I am.

1ST ATHLETE (*With a look at* 2ND ATHLETE)   Well . . . let's go back and give 'em the news.

2ND ATHLETE   O.K.
(*The two* ATHLETES *run off together.* BEN *stands rigid. The* OLD MAN *watches with keen and sympathetic interest. The cheering and the music resume in the background*)

OLD MAN (*Finally*)   It shouldn't frighten you so . . . to lose.

BEN   No . . . it *shouldn't.*
(TOM *and* ANN *come running on together.* ANN *calls*)

ANN   Ben!
(BEN *turns as if trying to escape them*)

TOM   Ben, we have to talk to you.
(BEN *waits. They come to his side*)

ANN   You knew? I'm wearing Tom's pin? (BEN *nods*) *I* wanted to be the one to tell you, Ben.

TOM   We were *both* gonna tell you, Ben.

ANN   Ben . . . (BEN *stands attentive but keeps his eyes off both of them*) I just wanted to tell you . . . I really like you an awful lot.

TOM   Ann still thinks the world of you, Ben . . . and I guess you know how I feel, don't you? *I* feel, we'll always be buddies.
(*He puts an arm around* BEN'S *shoulder*)

ANN   Tom says you're the best friend he ever had.

TOM   And I mean it.

ANN   I don't see any reason why we can't still be friends, Ben. Maybe better friends than before.

TOM   Ben—why don't you come to the Varsity with us tonight? If you don't have a date, you can dance with Ann all you want to . . .

ANN   I'd love it, Ben.

TOM   Come on, Ben. You'll get over this eventually. Why not now?

BEN   (*Words come with difficulty*)   I hadn't planned . . . to go to the Varsity.

VOICES (*Calling from the stadium*)   Tom! Hey, Tom! Where are you, Tom? Your event is next, Tom!

TOM   Golly, I'm next. I gotta beat it. Wait for me at the gate, Ann.
(TOM *starts, but* BEN *holds him*)

BEN (Grasping TOM's *sleeve*)   Tom!
(*He is trembling with rage*)

TOM   Hey, Ben, I gotta go.

BEN (*Sobbing in rage*)   Damn you, Tom! Damn you!
(*He seizes* TOM *by the throat*)

TOM (*Freeing himself from* BEN's *hold*)   Ben!

ANN   Ben, you can't hate Tom.

TOM (*Going to* BEN)   I don't want you to hate me, Ben.

BEN (*Realizing the futility of his gesture*)   Go on.

TOM   I don't want you to hate me, Ben.

BEN   Go on. They're waiting.
(TOM *runs off*)

ANN   You mustn't blame Tom for what happened, Ben. It's my fault as much as his. We've fallen in love. Don't you see? It wasn't something that we did intentionally. It . . . just happened.

BEN   I don't feel much like talking, Ann.

ANN   I understand. Please try to look on us as friends, Ben. Please.

BEN   I'm not sure I know how to look on anyone any more, Ann.

ANN   Just remember that we do like you. We do.

BEN   "Like"?

ANN   You'll find another girl in time, Ben. A girl who'll love you just as much as I love Tom.

BEN   Some people . . . don't find love . . . very easily, Ann.

ANN   In another few weeks you'll wonder what you ever saw in me.

BEN   Are you going to be married?

ANN   This summer. Oh, Ben, we want you as best man, and we want you as our friend forever. (*Kisses him on the cheek*) Goodbye, Ben.
(*She runs off.* BEN *slips to the ground, his body convulsed with groaning sobs, writhing in mortal agony. The* OLD MAN, *who has stood withdrawn on his hillock throughout all this scene, now makes a tentative gesture, as though hoping to console* BEN, *but then decides it might be better not to interfere, and so returns his attention to the field below where trumpets are sounding for a new event and the band plays "Boola Boola." But he cannot help recalling* BEN'S *prostrate body on the ground, and so he turns again from the games and goes to him, speaking softly*)

OLD MAN   Young man . . . (BEN *does not move*) You mustn't let yourself feel so deeply.

BEN   Now I know why people go mad and kill.

OLD MAN   Yes. Some people go mad and kill.

BEN (*In a fury of protest*)   I don't *want* to hate. I don't *want* to.

OLD MAN   No one wants to.

BEN (*Jumps to his feet, runs to the right, calling into the distance*)   Tom, come back! I won't hate you, Tom. I won't hate you.
(*Down in the stadium, a gun is fired starting the race*)

OLD MAN   He won't hear you now. He's in the race.

BEN (*In a weak voice, returning*)   Tom!

OLD MAN   Young man, maybe you'd like to come up on my hillock and watch.

BEN   No.

OLD MAN   Oh, the games are most exciting. Come and watch. Here beside me.

BEN   I've always played in the games. I feel humiliated just to stand and watch.

OLD MAN   Oh, come now. One doesn't have to run in the races to enjoy them. Sometimes I think I enjoy the relays more than anyone, standing up here on my lonely hillside. And I can spell *Nebuchadnezzar,* too. (*He chuckles.* BEN *is still reluctant*) Come along. (BEN *slowly rises and starts up the hillside, as though trying an unheard-of experiment. The* OLD MAN, *displays the view as though it were a great painting*) Up here, you can see them all, and the view gives them perspective. Isn't it a magnificent sight? (BEN *looks intently into the distance*) And when the games are over, you don't have to fight your way through all the crowd.

BEN (*With passive interest*)   Look! Tom won his race, didn't he?

OLD MAN   Yes. He won. He won. And now they're starting a new event. Oh, listen to the trumpets and

the bumptious band. And see the cheer leaders jumping up and down.
(*We hear these sounds*)

BEN Yes, it all looks very different, from a distance.

OLD MAN It's beautiful, isn't it? And exciting?

BEN Yes. From here, it's beautiful and exciting.
(*The band plays "Boola Boola" as the two men stare down in the distance*)

Curtain

ABOUT THE AUTHOR

Ever since his *Come Back, Little Sheba* caused the New York Drama Critics' Circle to acclaim him "the most promising new playwright of 1950," William Inge has been regarded as one of the most important American playwrights of the mid-century era.

In 1953, he received the Pulitzer Prize, the New York Drama Critics' Circle Award, and the Donaldson Award for *Picnic*. In 1955, *Bus Stop* was presented with even greater success than either of his previous plays; it ran for sixty weeks in New York and was then presented on tour by two separate companies. *The Dark at the Top of the Stairs* opened to critical applause in 1957. It was based on Inge's initial script, *Farther Off from Heaven,* which was brought to the attention of Margo Jones by Tennessee Williams, and was produced by Miss Jones at her famous Dallas Theatre in 1947. Inge's sixth play, *A Loss of Roses,* was presented on Broadway in 1959; and he received the Oscar for the best screenplay of 1961 for *Splendor in the Grass*.

William Inge was born in Independence, Kansas, graduated from the University of Kansas, and received an M.A. degree from George Peabody College. He taught in a high school in Columbus, Kansas, at Stephens College in Columbia, Missouri, and at Washington University in St. Louis. He has also been a radio newscaster in Wichita, Kansas, and a dramatic critic for the St. Louis *Star-Times*.

In neither the movie nor the Broadway version of *Picnic,* which won the Pulitzer Prize and the New York Drama Critics' Circle Award in 1953, did William Inge completely fulfill his original intention for the script. In August, 1962, *Summer Brave,* the final reworked version of *Picnic,* received this notice when it was presented in Hyde Park: "The characters remain the same, but a shift of emphasis toward the women makes an even more powerful drama than the original."

The one-act plays in this volume were written mostly in the early 1950's. In *People in the Wind* can be seen the beginnings of Mr. Inge's Broadway success *Bus Stop;* in some of the other plays are brief portraits which he later developed into full characterizations. *Bus Riley's Back in Town* has now been expanded to a full-length play.

With Mr. Inge's first Broadway play, *Come Back, Little Sheba,* critics considered him one of the most promising playwrights of the fifties. His other successes include *Bus Stop,* 1955, and *The Dark at the Top of the Stairs,* 1957, which was called Mr. Inge's finest play by Brooks Atkinson of the New York *Times,* and which received wide critical acclaim. His sixth play, *A Loss of Roses,* appeared in 1959, and in 1961 he received an Oscar for *Splendor in the Grass* as the best screenplay of that year.